CDF

CEDRIC D. FISHER & COMPANY
PUBLISHERS
WWW.CEDRICDFISHER.COM

ACKNOWLEDGMENTS

Thanks to the collaboration and family-friendly atmosphere of the people and organizations in the San Antonio area, the Bexar County School Boards Coalition shares valuable education information for our communities, the state of Texas, and our nation through this book. A special committee, comprised of Board of Trustees from current and past ISDs, determined the book's contents and structure. The team of Bobby Blount, Sandy Hughey, and Lisa Jackson prepared it for public release.

Layout & Graphic Design: Sandra Schwartzman - www.sswdesign.com
Publisher: Cedric D. Fisher & Company Publishers LLC - www.cedricdfisher.com

The Bexar County School Boards Coalition expresses gratitude to all the people and organizations that provided the data and information:

Claudia Barrientos, East Central ISD
Bryan Benway, Boerne ISD
Vanessa Barry, San Antonio ISD
Florinda Bernal, Southwest ISD
Dell Braziel, East Central ISD
Kim Cathey, Floresville ISD
Darren Calvert, Medina Valley ISD
Janice Carpio-Hernandez, Southwest ISD
Dell Claudia, East Central ISD
Sheila Collazo, Somerset ISD
Jennifer Collier, South San ISD
Stephen Enriquez, Education Service Center Region 20
Randy Escamilla, Southside ISD, Northside ISD
Monica Faulkenberry
Karen Freeman, Northside ISD
Natalie Guzman, Judson ISD
Janie Hatton, Fort Sam ISD

Eduardo Hernandez, Edgewood ISD
Tonya Hyde, Lackland ISD
Sandy Hughey, Northeast ISD
Lisa Jackson, Go Public
Ricardo Moreno, Harlandale ISD
Brandon Oliver, East Central ISD
Patti Pawlak-Perales, Alamo Heights ISD
Barry Perez, Northside ISD
Amelia Portillo, Edgewood ISD
Lou Ann Powers, Southside ISD
Sylvia Rincon, Southside ISD
Matty Salinas, Randolph Field ISD
Letticia Sever, Schertz-Cibolo-Universal City ISD
Eduardo Suarez, Schertz-Cibolo-Universal City ISD
Tyra Timmons, Fort Sam ISD
Mariana Veraza, Harlandale ISD
Willie White, Ft. Sam ISD

Special gratitude to our ISD and education partners:

Bexar County and San Antonio Area Superintendents
Bexar County and San Antonio Area Public Information Officers
Bexar County and San Antonio Area Trustees
Education Service Center Region 20
Go Public
Taft High School, Northside ISD
Texas Higher Education Coordinating Board
UP Partnership

We started the Bexar County School Boards Coalition fifteen years ago as a forum for the education Board of Trustees in the San Antonio area to establish peer relationships, collaborate on common challenges, share experiences, and advocate for all students.

In 2011, the Coalition released its first book "Public Education in Bexar County". The purpose of this book was to serve as the reference source for the facts and figures regarding the 20 Independent School Districts (ISDs) in the San Antonio area. "Public Education in Bexar County" was distributed to policy makers, public institutions, educators, and the public. Almost a decade later, the Coalition felt the time was right to release a second book. Our original goal was to share the positive information and stories about our ISDs. We had no idea that a pandemic would occur in the middle of us drafting the book. The pandemic really highlighted the critical and multiple roles that our ISDs have in the mental, emotional, and physiological daily needs of our students and the community. Thus, while "Public Education in the San Antonio Area" started out to tell the story about education in one large metropolitan area, it really tells stories that are applicable to school districts across our nation.

On behalf of the Trustees in the San Antonio area, I wanted to include a note of gratitude for all the educators across our great nation. We express our thanks to each of them for what they have and continue to do for our students. We have always known about the commitment and sacrifices that educators have made through the years, but no one could have imagined what they have faced and triumphed over in 2020. The only way I know to express our gratitude in words is to reference the lyrics from a well-known song: "You are the wind beneath my wings".

We hope that everyone enjoys our story.

TABLE OF CONTENTS

INDEPENDENT SCHOOL DISTRICTS PAGES

CHAPTER ONE

INTRODUCTION TO THE BEXAR COUNTY INDEPENDENT SCHOOL DISTRICTS (ISDs)

INTRODUCTION TO THE BEXAR COUNTY INDEPENDENT SCHOOL DISTRICTS (ISDs)

(Data provided by: Education Service Center (ESC), Region 20, Texas Higher Education Coordinating Board (THECB), and UP Partnership.)

As stated in the Texas Education Code, the mission of the Texas public education system is to ensure that all Texas children have access to a quality education that enables them to achieve their potential and fully participate now and in the future in the social, economic, and educational opportunities of our state and nation (1). The Texas Constitution further delineates, "That mission is grounded on the conviction that a general diffusion of knowledge is essential for the welfare of this state and for the preservation of the liberties and rights of citizens" (2). The school districts and charter schools created in accordance with the laws of this state have the primary responsibility for implementing the state's system of public education and ensuring student performance in accordance with this code (3).

Texas has 1,023 public school districts and 177 charter operations. Most of the school districts are independent school districts (ISDs); some are consolidated school districts (CSDs); and one is a municipal school district. "Independent" means that the school district is separate from any municipality, county, or state, i.e., the school district has its own taxing authority outside the direct control of other governmental entities (4).

At its peak, Bexar County included over 50 ISDs. Presently, the Texas Education Agency (TEA) identifies 15 ISDs as being in Bexar County. These 15 ISDs were formed as follows:

• As shown in Figure 1, two of the current fifteen Bexar County ISDs divested from other districts: Edgewood divested from Bexar County School and South San divested from Edgewood

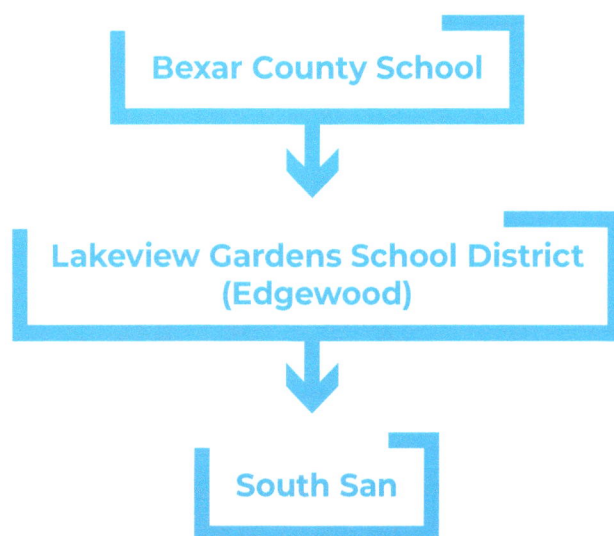

```
          Bexar County School
                  |
                  v
    Lakeview Gardens School District
             (Edgewood)
                  |
                  v
             South San
```

Figure 1. Divested School Systems

INTRODUCTION TO THE BEXAR COUNTY INDEPENDENT SCHOOL DISTRICTS (ISDs)

• As shown in Figure 2, eight of the current fifteen Bexar County ISDs were created through consolidation of districts or independent schools: East Central consolidated 24 districts, Judson consolidated 3, North East consolidated 7, Northside consolidated 12, San Antonio consolidated 3, Somerset consolidated 5, Southside consolidated 6, and Southwest consolidated 5. The CSDs that were consolidated to form Comal and Schertz-Cibolo-Universal City ISDs are included in Figure 2.

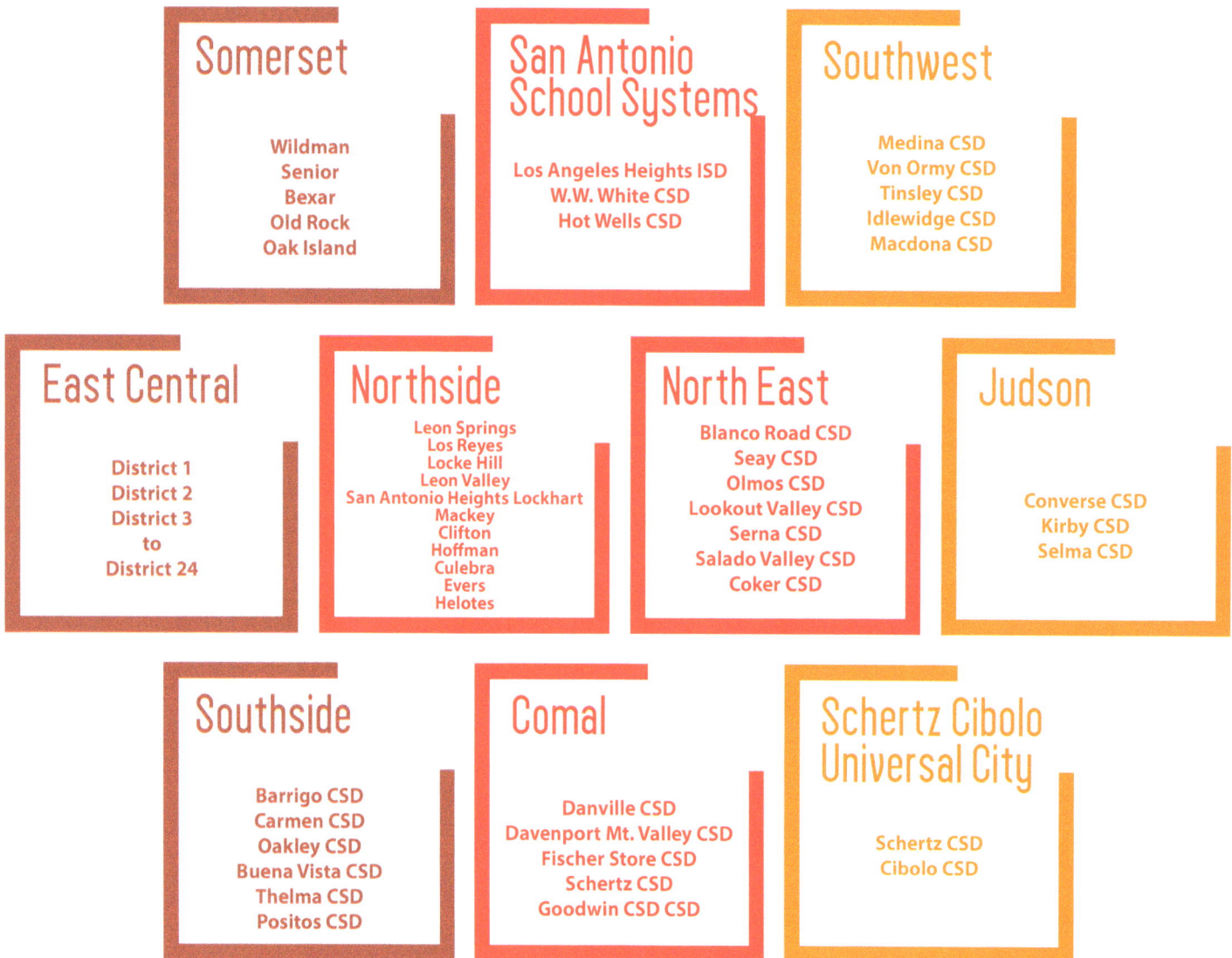

Somerset
Wildman
Senior
Bexar
Old Rock
Oak Island

San Antonio School Systems
Los Angeles Heights ISD
W.W. White CSD
Hot Wells CSD

Southwest
Medina CSD
Von Ormy CSD
Tinsley CSD
Idlewidge CSD
Macdona CSD

East Central
District 1
District 2
District 3
to
District 24

Northside
Leon Springs
Los Reyes
Locke Hill
Leon Valley
San Antonio Heights Lockhart
Mackey
Clifton
Hoffman
Culebra
Evers
Helotes

North East
Blanco Road CSD
Seay CSD
Olmos CSD
Lookout Valley CSD
Serna CSD
Salado Valley CSD
Coker CSD

Judson
Converse CSD
Kirby CSD
Selma CSD

Southside
Barrigo CSD
Carmen CSD
Oakley CSD
Buena Vista CSD
Thelma CSD
Positos CSD

Comal
Danville CSD
Davenport Mt. Valley CSD
Fischer Store CSD
Schertz CSD
Goodwin CSD CSD

Schertz Cibolo Universal City
Schertz CSD
Cibolo CSD

Figure 2. Consolidated School Systems

Five ISDs are partially located in Bexar County. These ISDs are not identified by TEA with Bexar County since most of their student enrollment is in counties surrounding Bexar County. Nevertheless, the Board of Trustees in these 5 ISDs are included as members in the Bexar County School Boards Coalition along with the Board of Trustees of the 15 ISDs in Bexar County.

CREATION DATES

The creation dates for the 20 ISDs are shown in Figure 3. All 20 ISDs report demographic, student performance, financial, staffing, programmatic, discipline, and other data to the State. This data is reported publicly and can be disaggregated to the following categories: campuses, districts, region, and state (5).

1888
Harlandale
ISD

1903
San Antonio
ISD

1907
Boerne
ISD

1909
Alamo Heights
ISD

1913
Southside
ISD

1922
South San
ISD

Somerset
ISD

1929
Floresville
ISD

1933
Randolph Field
ISD

1949
Northside
ISD

East Central
ISD

1950
Edgewood
ISD

North East
ISD

1951
Fort Sam
Houston
ISD

Southwest
ISD

1953
Lackland
ISD

1956
Comal
ISD

1958
Judson
ISD

1959
Medina Valley
ISD

1961
Schertz Cibolo
Universal City
ISD

Figure 3. Creation Dates

ENROLLMENT BY RACE/ETHNICITY

Table 1 shows the percentage of Bexar County students enrolled by their identified race/ethnicity. This percentage is contrasted to the state average. Texas has approximately 5.5 million students, including 5.2 million in ISDs and 300,000 in charter systems (6). Bexar county has 375,000 students, which is 7% of the state enrollment.

Student Group	State	Bexar County
Hispanic	52.6%	68%
White	27.4%	20%
African American	12.6%	7%
Asian	4.5%	2%
2 + Races	2.4%	3%

Table 1. Bexar County and State Ethnicity/Race Enrollment

ENROLLMENT BY GRADE LEVEL

Figure 4 shows the percentage of students enrolled in Bexar County schools by grade level. In Texas, 27% of all students are enrolled in high schools, 21% in middle schools, 48% in elementary schools, and 4% in combined elementary and secondary schools (7). In Bexar County, 29% of all students are enrolled in high schools, 22% in middle schools, and 49% in elementary schools.

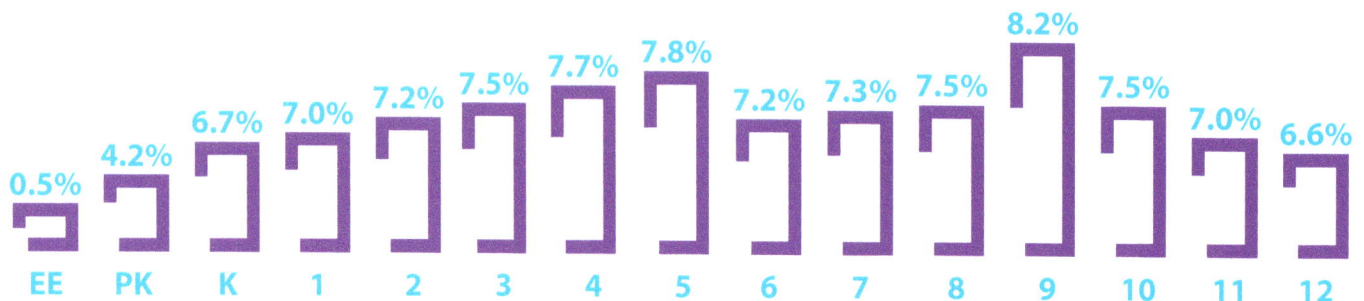

EE	PK	K	1	2	3	4	5	6	7	8	9	10	11	12
0.5%	4.2%	6.7%	7.0%	7.2%	7.5%	7.7%	7.8%	7.2%	7.3%	7.5%	8.2%	7.5%	7.0%	6.6%

Figure 4. Bexar County Grade Enrollment

STUDENTS BY PROGRAM

Figure 5 shows the percentage of students enrolled in student identified programs. Bexar County ISDs have a higher percentage in the Special Education Program than the state average and a lower percentage in the Bilingual Program. In Texas, 18.8% of students are in the Bilingual program, 25.8% in Career and Technical Education (CTE) program, 7.9 % in Gifted and Talented (G&T) program, and 9.2% in Special Education program (8). In Bexar County, 7% of students are in the bilingual program, 25% in CTE program, 7% in G&T program, and 11% in Special Education program.

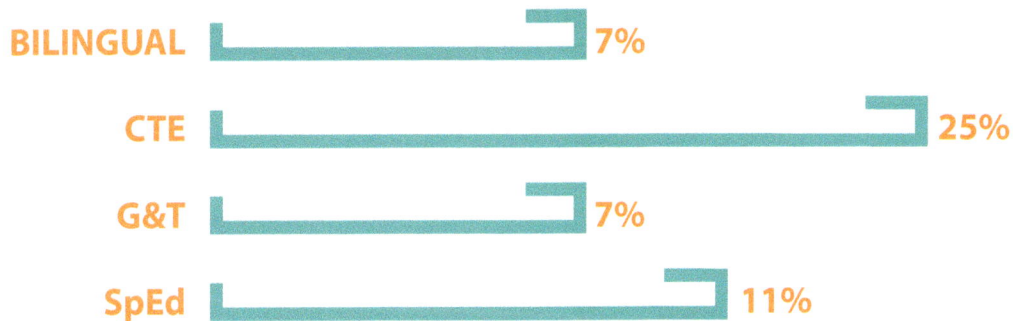

BILINGUAL _____ 7%

CTE _____ 25%

G&T _____ 7%

SpEd _____ 11%

Figure 5. Bexar County Student Programs Enrollment

STUDENTS IDENTIFIED AS ECONOMICALLY DISADVANTAGED

Figure 6 shows the categories for the 57% of students identified as economically disadvantaged in Bexar County. In Texas, between 2008-09 and 2018-19, the percentage increase in the number of students identified as economically disadvantaged increased by 22.5% (9).

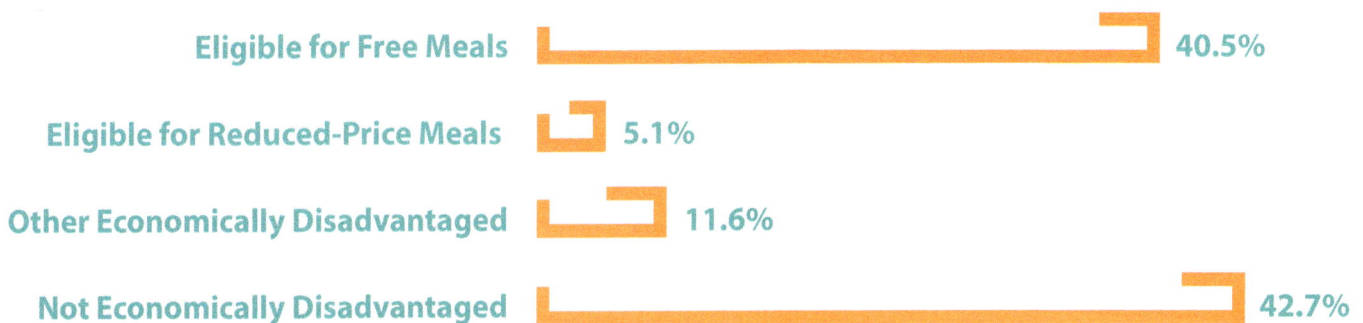

Eligible for Free Meals _____ 40.5%

Eligible for Reduced-Price Meals __ 5.1%

Other Economically Disadvantaged __ 11.6%

Not Economically Disadvantaged _____ 42.7%

Figure 6. Bexar County Economically Disadvantaged Student Identification Categories

CRADLE TO CAREER OUTCOMES

"Cradle to Career Outcomes" highlight student outcomes across the education pipeline to assess how students are progressing throughout the county. Table 2 shows the Cradle to Career Outcomes for Bexar County including: Kindergarten Readiness, 3rd Grade Reading Achievement, 8th Grade Math Achievement, High School Graduation, Postsecondary Enrollment, and Postsecondary Completion (10).

	All Students	African American	American Indian	Asian	Latin	Multiracial	Pacific Islander	White	Economically Disadvantaged	English Language Learner	Females	Males
Kindergarten Readiness 1	47%	42%	N/A	53%	43%	53%	N/A	60%	40%	44%	Not Collected	Not Collected
3rd Grade Reading 2	40%	33%	N/A	59%	36%	52%	59%	58%	31%	39%	43%	38%
8th Grade Math 3	53%	44%	52%	80%	49%	65%	71%	69%	44%	35%	55%	50%
College Ready 4	47%	34%	73%	74%	42%	60%	58%	65%	35%	24%	50%	43%
High School Graduation 5	91%	89%	95%	96%	90%	93%	90%	95%	93%	79%	94%	89%
Postsecondary Enrollment 6	54%	49%	71%	73%	52%	63%	66%	59%	47%	34%	60%	47%
Postsecondary Completion (4-yr) 7	45%	43%	44%	41%	46%	41%	17%	45%	Not Collected	Not Collected	50%	40%
Postsecondary Completion (2-yr) 7	28%	22%	N/A	37%	29%	35%	33%	26%	Not Collected	Not Collected	31%	24%

Table 2. Cradle to Career Outcomes for Students in Bexar County
(Source: UP Partnership, Interwoven Futures Activating Strategic Alignment for Youth Success)

NUMBER OF SCHOOLS

Figure 7 shows the number of schools in Bexar County. In Texas, there are 8,759 schools, including 8,054 in ISDs and 705 in charters (11). In Bexar County, there are 543 schools. The schools identified as DAEP/JJAEP and Alternative includes elementary, middle, and high schools. Their enrollment consists of students removed from their regular campus for mandatory or discretionary disciplinary reasons.

321	90	65	26	41
Elementary	Middle	High	Alternative	DAEP/JAEP

Figure 7. Bexar County Number of Schools

SCHOOL PERFORMANCE

Figure 8 shows the performance rating for schools in Bexar County. In Texas, 89.3% of schools were rated as Met Standard, 3.9% as Improvement Required, and 6.8% as Not Rated (12). In Bexar County, 84% of schools were rated as Met Standard, 7% of schools as Improvement Required, 8% as Not Rated, and 1% as Met Alternative Standard.

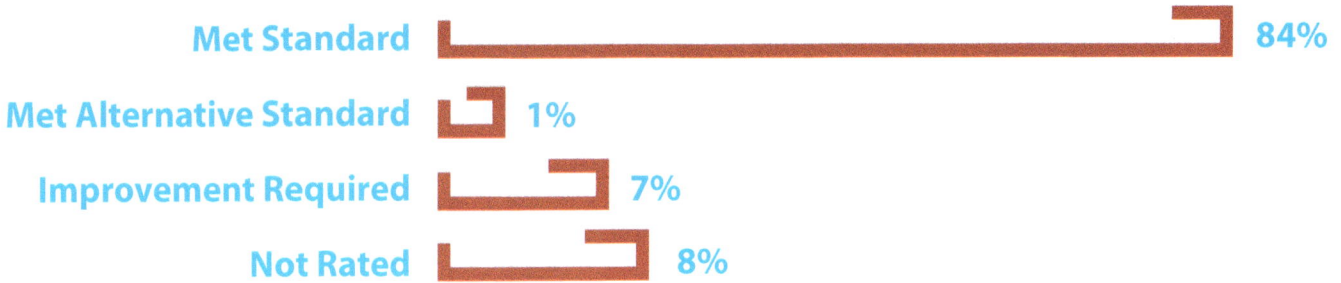

Met Standard	84%
Met Alternative Standard	1%
Improvement Required	7%
Not Rated	8%

Figure 8. Bexar County Performance Ratings for Schools

EMPLOYMENT

Figure 9 shows the percentage of employees by position that are employed in Bexar County ISDs. As the second largest employment group in San Antonio, the Bexar County ISDs employ approximately 50,000 individuals. Half of these employees are teachers while the other half includes office secretaries, food service staff, bus drivers, IT staff, academic specialists, maintenance staff, administrators, and other employer categories.

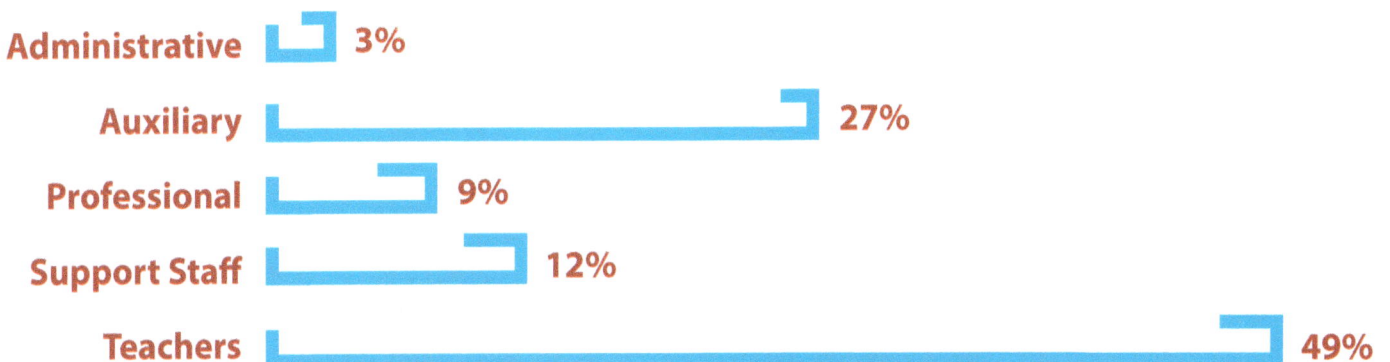

Administrative	3%
Auxiliary	27%
Professional	9%
Support Staff	12%
Teachers	49%

Figure 9. Bexar County Percentage of Employees by Positions

BUDGET REVENUE

Figure 10 shows the percentage of revenue received by the Bexar County ISDs from local, state, and federal sources. Local funding for Texas public schools is generated primarily by property tax levied on local taxable values. State funding is generated from the General Revenue-Related (GRR) funds, including the General Revenue Fund, Available School Fund, State Technology and Instructional Materials Fund, and the Foundation School General Revenue Dedicated Account (13). Bexar County ISDs received 12% of funds from federal sources, 36% from the state, and 52% from local.

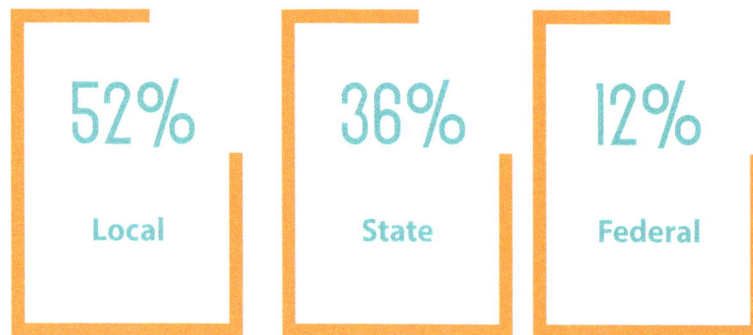

52%	36%	12%
Local	State	Federal

Figure 10. Bexar County ISDs Revenue Sources

BUDGET EXPENDITURE

Figure 11 shows three of the categories for the $3.6 billion expenditures by the Bexar County ISDs. The highest expenditure category is instruction. The extra-curricular and administration expenditures are less than 3% each of the total expenditures.

Expenditures by Category			
Administration	$	88,587,512.00	2.5% of total
Extra-Curricular	$	95,296,492.00	2.6% of total
Instruction	$	2,040,178,340.00	56.6% of total
Other Categories	$	1,377,563,379 .00	38.3% of total
Total Expenditures	$	3,601,625,723.00	

Figure 11. Bexar County ISDs Funding Expenditures

HIGHER EDUCATION 8TH GRADE COHORT

Figure 12 shows the Texas Higher Education Coordinating Board (THECB) 8th grade cohort data for Bexar County ISDs. THECB tracks education outcomes for cohorts of students who attend 8th grade in a Texas public school including rates of high school graduation, higher education enrollment, as well as types of degrees earned from a Texas college or university. The data only includes 48 percent of the 8th grade students.

	African American	Hispanic	White	Others
Cohort of students reported in 8th	2,047	14,479	4,946	947
8th grade cohort reported enrolled in 9th	91%	93%	93%	92%
8th grade cohort reported enrolled in10th	78%	78%	84%	87%
Reported as high school graduates	72%	75%	79%	81%
Enrolled TX 4-year and 2-year	51%	49%	61%	65%
Earned an associate, baccalaureate or above degree or a certificate from a Coordinating Board-approved program	18%	17%	34%	41%

Figure 12. 8th Grader Cohort Longitudinal Data
* In the TEA enrollment snapshot, fall collection

HIGHER EDUCATION SCHOOLS ATTENDED

Figure 13 shows the percentage of students from Bexar County that enrolled in a higher education institution in the San Antonio area. Approximately, half of these students attended one of the Alamo Colleges. Among the universities, at 14%, UTSA had the highest percentage of students enrolled from a Bexar County ISD. The chart shows the colleges and universities with at least 3% enrollment from students that attended a Bexar County ISD.

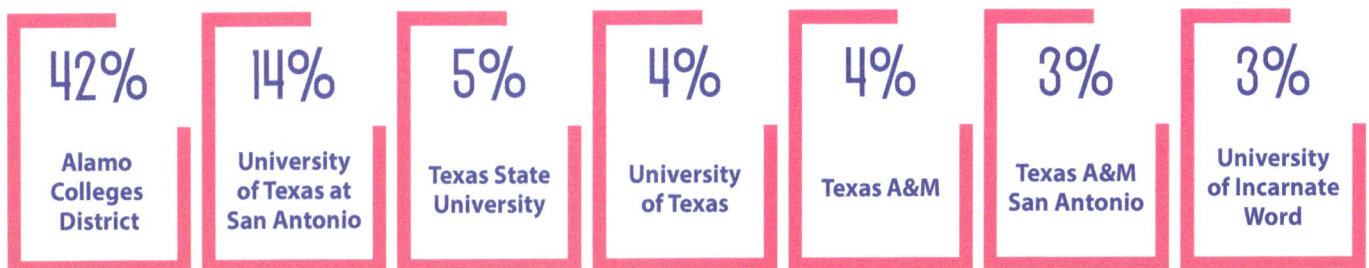

42%	14%	5%	4%	4%	3%	3%
Alamo Colleges District	University of Texas at San Antonio	Texas State University	University of Texas	Texas A&M	Texas A&M San Antonio	University of Incarnate Word

Total enrolled: 10,071 Not found: 11,116

Figure 13. San Antonio Higher Education Enrollment by Local Students

CHAPTER TWO

DISTRICT STORIES

ALAMO HEIGHTS ISD, est. 1909

District Mission

The Alamo Heights Independent School District, the heart of our community whose passion is excellence, will educate and empower every student to excel academically and as a confident, compassionate citizen with impeccable character and a global perspective through engaging, personally challenging, and relevant experiences that inspire learning for life.

District Highlights

• Jeff Wheatcraft, Alamo Heights Junior School STEM Teacher, Trinity Prize Winner, named Texas Teacher of the Year in 2018
• Named Best Small School District in Texas by H-E-B Excellence in Education Awards
• New Heights Business Incubator Program has highest initial enrollment in the country
• Destination Imagination students make it to Globals annually
• Named a Recognized Unified Champion School by Special Olympics Texas and a National Banner School by Special Olympics North America
• Rocketry Program has earned 4 Diamond Goddard Awards
• Spanish Immersion, Dual Language, Gifted/Talented, and Special Education Programs considered among the best in the region
• Superintendent Dr. Dana Bashara received one of San Antonio Business Journal's Women's Leadership Awards

DISTRICT STORY

At AHISD, students are at the center of every decision. Our goal is to prepare our students for the future and create a learning experience where each student thrives. In an ever evolving and advancing world, AHISD strives to accord its students with the skills necessary for a successful and balanced life.

The AHISD Profile of a Learner depicts all that we, as a district, embody. Profile of a Learner provides teachers with a roadmap to create learning experiences for students. The goal is that each student will bloom into an individual ready for his or her personal future. With the district in the fifth year of the "responsible rollout," we have over 300 Engaged Classrooms across the district. These new environments are learner-centered workplaces with a collaborative culture where students are at work. With the Profile of a Learner as a driving force, these classrooms focus on communication, creativity, digital literacy, critical thinking, and problem-solving.

As a district, we understand that ongoing support for our teachers is key to making these classrooms a success. Each teacher works alongside an instructional coach. Together, they align their work with teaching best practices, future-ready skills, and the Profile of Learner. The Engaged Classroom teachers focus on creating learning experiences using the Blueprint for Learning framework. This blueprint encourages teachers to consider all aspects of the Profile of a Learner. With the Profile of a Learner as our roadmap, our district is committed to preparing our students to become active, successful, and contributing members of society.

DEMOGRAPHICS

Student Enrollment: 4,810 Students

Student Demographics:
- African American: 2.3 %
- Asian: 3.8%
- Hispanic: 41%
- Native American: 0.4%
- Pacific Islander: 0.1%
- White: 51.4%
- Two or more races: 1%
- Economically Disadvantaged: 20.6%

Number of Schools: 6
Total Employees: 604
Student/Teacher Ratio: 13.9
Average Student Expenditure: $10,042

HOW TO REACH US

7101 Broadway, San Antonio, Texas 78209

210-824-2483 | Fax: 210-822-2221
info@ahisd.net | www.ahisd.net

iTunes App: AHISD
Twitter: @AHISD
Facebook: @AHISD
Instagram: @alamoheightsisd
YouTube: Alamo Heights Mules

BOERNE ISD, est. 1907

WE ARE BOERNE

District Mission
The Boerne Independent School District engages, inspires, and enriches our community through innovative learning experiences.

District Beliefs
• All students have talents and gifts and deserve the highest quality education
• All students should have opportunities to achieve high levels of success
• Children matter to the community and should experience a sense of belonging
• Children grow best with family and community nurturing
• All students must be post-high school ready to enter the workforce and/or higher education
• In educating the whole child by addressing not only academics but social/emotional needs
• Education is a partnership involving students, families, community, and the district

District Highlights
• 2019-20 Best Small School District in Texas by the HEB Excellence in Education Committee
• 2020 Top Workplace by the San Antonio Express-News
• Fair Oaks Ranch Elementary School was named a National Showcase School by Capturing Kids Hearts for the second straight year.
• Both Boerne High School and Champion High School were ranked as two of the top high schools in the San Antonio Region.
• One of the fastest-growing school districts in Texas (2019 Demographic Study)
• Largest employer in the community.
• Two consecutive TEA "A" Ratings
• Board selected as Best in the Region
• Named to the AP District Honor Roll by the College Board
• Received the Best Communities for Music Education designation

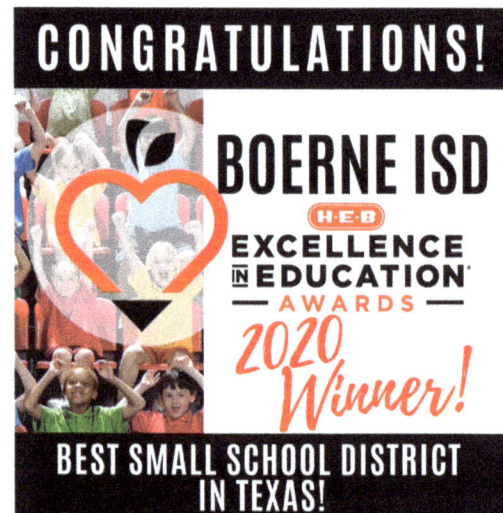

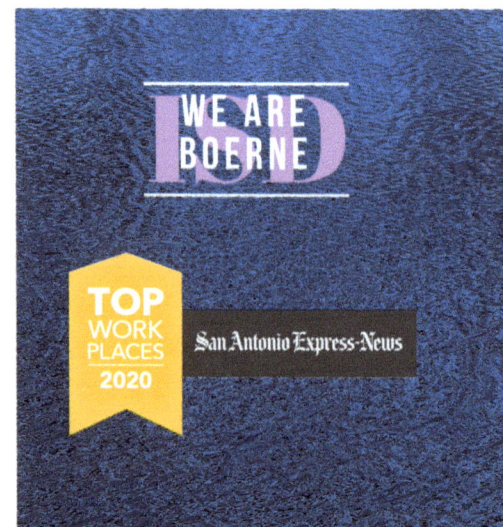

CONGRATULATIONS! BOERNE ISD H-E-B EXCELLENCE IN EDUCATION AWARDS 2020 Winner! BEST SMALL SCHOOL DISTRICT IN TEXAS!

WE ARE BOERNE TOP WORK PLACES 2020 San Antonio Express-News

DISTRICT STORY

Boerne ISD has had success in the classroom, as well as with extracurricular activities. In addition to being named 2019-20 Best Small School District in Texas by the HEB Excellence in Education Committee and a 2020 Top Workplace by the San Antonio Express-News, Fair Oaks Ranch Elementary School was named a National Showcase School by Capturing Kids Hearts for the second straight year. Both Boerne High School and Champion High School were ranked as two of the top high schools in the San Antonio Region. Herff Elementary Assistant Principal Beth Miller was named Texas Elementary Principals and Supervisors Association's Region 20 Assistant Principal of the Year. The Boerne-Champion Girls Cross Country Team won the 2019 Class 5-A State Championship, while the Champion Football team advanced to the State Semifinals, the best finish ever for a Boerne ISD football team.

Vision
Our community will engage students and adults in a challenging educational environment that inspires creativity and enriches lives for today's realities and tomorrow's possibilities. Engage. Inspire. Enrich.

Core Values
Boerne ISD, its faculty and staff, stand on a foundation of integrity, firm in the belief that our core values - Respect, Accountability, Perseverance, Service, and Compassion act as pillars that support our goal of achieving excellence in all that we do.

DEMOGRAPHICS

Student Enrollment: 9,611 Students

Student Demographics:
- African American: 0.8 %
- Asian: 1.1%
- Hispanic: 30.3%
- Native American: 0.3%
- Pacific Islander: 0.1%
- White: 65.2%
- Two or more races: 2.2%
- Economically Disadvantaged: 17.3%

Number of Schools: 12
Total Employees: 1,300
Student/Teacher Ratio: 16.2
Average Student Expenditure: $8,540

HOW TO REACH US

235 Johns Rd., Boerne, Texas 78006

830-357-2000

communications@boerne- isd.net

Twitter: @BoerneISD
Facebook: @BoerneISD
Instagram: @boerneISD

EAST CENTRAL ISD, est. 1949

District Mission
Together, we will customize learning experiences so that every student is continuously challenged to advance their knowledge and ability in every classroom, in every school, every day.

District Beliefs
East Central ISD aims to cultivate literate problem-solvers who are prepared to thrive in an interconnected world with a dynamic economy. We envision an inclusive, exceptional school system that teaches all children to read critically, write compellingly, think logically, and solve problems creatively. We value diversity, customer service, personal accountability, fiscal responsibility, adaptability, collaboration, and loyalty.

District Highlights
• All-day prekindergarten available at all elementary schools including a tuition-based option
• After school programs
• Dual credit & AP courses
• Standards-based learning & grading
• Service-learning opportunities
• CAST Lead campus (focuses on leadership positions in the retail, hospitality, tourism, and e-commerce industries)
• East Central Leadership Academy (choice school for elementary level)
• Dual language program Pre-K through 12th
• Career and Technical Education (CTE) industry certifications
• State-of-the-art Performing Arts Center
• Over 100 diverse clubs and programs at ECHS
• Nationally recognized FFA, fine arts, culinary arts and JROTC programs
• Community-Based Accountability System (CBAS)

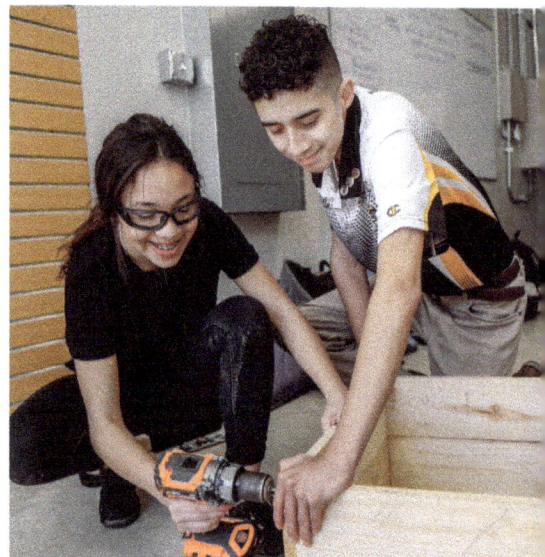

DISTRICT STORY

Established in 1949, East Central Independent School District's core business is growth, vision, and mission for every minute, every student, every day. Committed to a quality education, the District strives to promote a positive school climate that optimizes teaching and learning in accordance with the values of its community. Creating dynamic problem-solvers for a diverse, global economy, through an engaging curriculum, is of paramount importance to ECISD which has a current enrollment of 10,215 students.

East Central ISD has significant traditional roots yet blended with modern techniques. This approach results in well-rounded students. We seek inclusive, collaborative partnerships in our community and we utilize our resources responsibly. Our high-performing engaged workforce produces a positive teaching and learning environment for our students.

DEMOGRAPHICS

Student Enrollment: 10,215 Students

Student Demographics:
· African American: 8.2%
· Asian: 0.5%
· Hispanic: 74.4%
· Native American: 0.1%
· Pacific Islander: 0.1%
· White: 15.2%
· Two or more races: 1.5%
· Economically Disadvantaged: 64.9%

Number of Schools: 11
Total Employees: 1,312
Student/Teacher Ratio: 16.5
Avg Student Expenditure: $8,547

HOW TO REACH US

East Central ISD, 6634 New Sulphur Springs Road, San Antonio, Texas 78263

210-634-6100 | Fax: 210-648-0931
marcom@ecisd.net
www.ecisd.net

App: East Central ISD through Google Play or Apple Store
Twitter: @ecisdtweets
Facebook: @ECProud
LinkedIn: ECproud

EDGEWOOD
INDEPENDENT ◊ SCHOOL ◊ DISTRICT
San Antonio
PROFESSIONALISM ◊ ACCOUNTABILITY ◊ COMMUNICATION

District Mission

Edgewood ISD provides an exceptional learning experience that engages, empowers, and prepares students to compete and reach their highest potential in an ever-changing world.

District Highlights

Five Innovation Zones
- Leadership
- Fine Arts
- STEAM
- Early Childhood
- Public Service

Innovation Schools
- Brentwood STEAM School of Innovation
- Gardendale Early Learning Program, in partnership withPre-K 4 SA
- Las Palmas Leadership School for Girls
- Gus Garcia University School, in partnership with Texas A&M University San Antonio
- Burleson School for Innovation and Education, in partnership with Texas A&M University San Antonio
- STEAM @ Perales Elementary
- Two Early College High Schools at John F. Kennedy and Memorial High School
- All-day Pre-K and Head Start classes

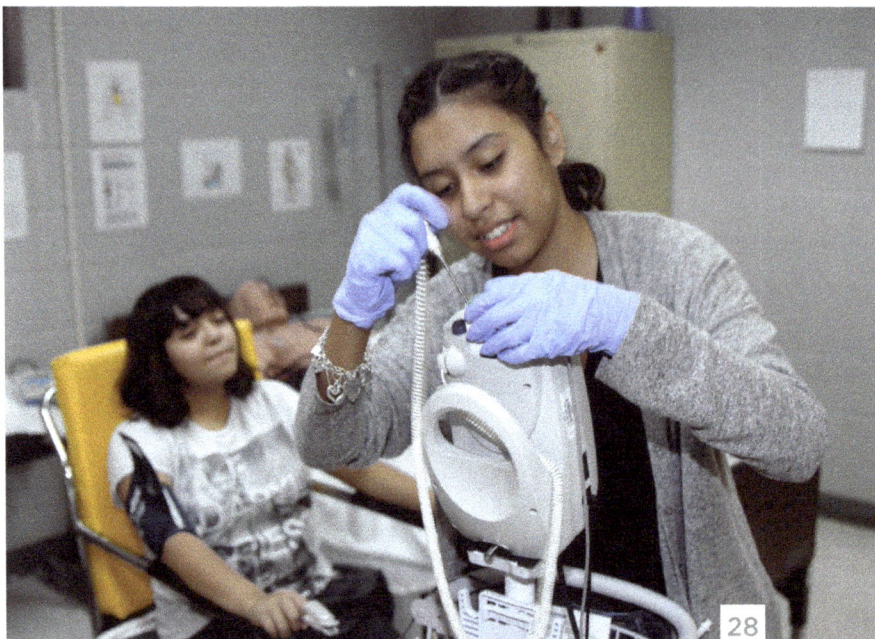

28

After-school programs
- Athletics
- Chess
- Robotics
- Services to improve families' education
- Family Leadership Institute
- Parent University
- F.A.C.E
(Family and Community Engagement) Chat
- Dual Language Courses
- All elementary campuses with the exception of STEAM @Perales Elementary
- Two Early Childhood Centers
- Gus Garcia University School

District Values
- Focus on Student Success
- Focus on Students and Families
- Focus on Operational Excellence
- Focus on Employee and Organizational Improvement
- Focus on Financial Stewardship

DEMOGRAPHICS

Student Enrollment: 10,467 Students

Student Demographics:
- African American: 1.5%
- Asian: 0.3%
- Hispanic: 97.4%
- Native American: 0%
- Pacific Islander: 0%
- White: 0.6%
- Two or more races: 0.1%
- Economically Disadvantaged: 93.2%

Number of Schools: 22
Total Employees: 1,580
Student/Teacher Ratio: 15.9
Average Student Expenditure: $10,890

DISTRICT STORY

Edgewood Independent School District is located on the west side of San Antonio, Texas. Today, over 20 schools and programs with over 10,000 students call Edgewood home. Even though the present Edgewood ISD became "independent" in January 1950, its formation can be traced back to 1905. Each generation remembers Edgewood differently from the next, but one universal truth remains...

"I've never experienced a more supportive community. I love how everyone is involved in everything."
Mikayla, John F. Kennedy High School

HOW TO REACH US

5358 West Commerce St, San Antonio, Texas 78237

210-444-4500 | Fax: 210-444-4525
www.eisd.net

Twitter: @EISDofSA
Facebook: @eisdofsa
YouTube: @EISDofSA

FLORESVILLE ISD, est. 1929

District Mission

FISD is committed to developing 21st century graduates who are life-long learners that are purposeful, innovative, collaborative, and possess character traits that lead to success.

District Goals

• Each student will maximize their potential
• Each student will be a life-long learner, prepared for their future
• Each student will be a contributing member of the global society
• FISD will strive to build strong relationships with stakeholders
• FISD will exercise fiscal responsibility

District Highlights

• Dual Language program serves over 200 elementary and middle school students
• Invites any student to participate in rich and rigorous learning by offering Advanced and Dual Credit courses
• Provides innovative learning environments that include providing every student a device for digital engagement
• STEM courses that focus on high-tech skills that are valuable in today's job market
• Partnership with Alamo Area Academies provides students with courses and certifications in Aerospace, Information Technology and Security, Advanced Technology and Manufacturing, Health Professions, and Heavy Equipment
• Students earn an average of 125 industry certifications in Welding, Automotive, Culinary Arts and Floral Design and other areas
• Challenge students mentally and physically. Students have opportunities in the areas of sports, music, art, drama, dance, video production, FFA, JROTC and many more

DISTRICT STORY

The Floresville Independent School District encompasses a geographic area of over 285 square miles in Wilson County, extending into southeast Bexar County, and is home to over 4,000 students.

Floresville offers a big city education in a small, hometown environment. FISD believes that collaboration between community, schools and family is the foundation of success for their students.

FISD educates the whole child. While offering exceptional academic options in Dual Language, Career and Technology Education, Advanced Academics and Dual Credit, FISD also focuses on students' emotional and social well-being. Preparing students for a prosperous life at FISD means providing engaging, rigorous learning opportunities, identifying strengths, exploring passions and learning the importance of contributing to the greater good.

DEMOGRAPHICS

Student Enrollment: 4,049 Students

Student Demographics:
• African American: 1.2%
• Asian: 0.5%
• Hispanic: 66.4%
• Native American: 0.3%
• Pacific Islander: .3%
• White: 29.5%
• Two or more races: 1.9%
• Economically Disadvantaged: 53.4%

Number of Schools: 5
Total Employees: 550
Student/Teacher Ratio: 16.4
Avg Student Expenditure: $6,160

HOW TO REACH US

1200 5th Street, Floresville, Texas 78114

830-393-5300 | Fax: 830-393-5399
info@fisd.us

Twitter: @floresvilleisd
Facebook: @floresville
Instagram: floresville_isd

FORT SAM HOUSTON, est. 1951

Fort Sam Houston ISD

District Highlights

Fort Sam Houston ISD is a consistent leader in student achievement and performance. Honors include: HEB Excellence in Education Award for Best Small School District and the Military Child Education Coalition Exemplary Partnership Award. Elementary students participate in a variety of programs to meet their academic needs and interests, including full day pre-kindergarten, STEM-based IMAGINASIUM experiences, elementary art, music and theatre arts classes, and extracurricular Robotics Clubs. Secondary students participate in JROTC, Photography, Journalism, Culinary Arts, Coding, Sports Medicine, Computer Programming, Media Design, and Video Design courses. We have won regional and state competitions in numerous UIL athletic and academic events and have earned appointments to the various military academies. Our students admitted to top-tier colleges and universities, received National Merit Scholarships, and named Presidential Scholars.

District Mission

The mission of the Fort Sam Houston ISD is to develop the hearts and minds of all students, empowering them to become successful, active contributors in a changing global community.

District Beliefs

• We exist to serve the military child
• We are a family of lifelong learners who respect and honor individual differences, diversity, and talent
• We believe a safe and caring environment fosters the emotional and social well-being of students
• We believe that every teacher is a leader; every leader is a teacher
• We inspire our students to their highest level of learning
• We, the school community, provide engaging, challenging, and meaningful work for learners
• We prepare students to be leaders by instilling character, competence, and creativity

Vision

Our vision is to promote a quality education, where every student is a learner, every learner is a graduate, and every graduate is a success.

DISTRICT STORY

Created in 1951, the Fort Sam Houston Independent School District is located on the sprawling Joint-Base San Antonio-Fort Sam Houston (JBSA) in northeast San Antonio, Texas. Created as a "special purpose district," FSHISD is an Independent School District, not a Department of Defense school. It is one of only seven districts in the United States whose boundaries are coterminous with the military installations they serve.

Annually serving approximately 1,600 school-age military dependents who reside on JBSA and Camp Bullis, the district is committed to providing an outstanding educational opportunity for all students to prepare them to become successful, responsible, and productive citizens.

FHISD takes pride in being a leader in student achievement and performance. FSHISD students have been recognized at the local, state, and national levels in areas of academic achievement and performance.

DEMOGRAPHICS

Student Enrollment: 1,612 Students

Student Demographics:
- African American: 16.9 %
- Asian: 2.5%
- Hispanic: 31.3%
- Native American: 0.7%
- Pacific Islander: 1.0%
- White: 37.7%
- Two or more races: 10%%
- Economically Disadvantaged: 29.6%

Number of Schools: 2
Total Employees: 278
Student/Teacher Ratio: 12.2
Average Student Expenditure: $14,114

HOW TO REACH US

4005 Winans Rd San Antonio, Texas 78234

210-368-8700
www.fshisd.net

Twitter: @FSHISD
Facebook: @FSHISD
Instagram: @fshisd
YouTube: FSHISD

HARLANDALE ISD, est. 1888

District Mission

HISD is a family working together to create a high-quality education where all students graduate to become productive and successful citizens for the 21st century.

District Goals

Provides staff development programs that prepare our employees to provide an exemplary teaching and learning environment. Foster a culture that prepares students for higher education and work-force readiness. Effectively and efficiently use all district resources to maintain sound fiscal policies and practices. Create innovative instructional facilities that engage the evolving needs of our students.

District Highlights

• Every college bound HISD high school graduate is awarded a $625 or $1,250 scholarship from the Harlandale Education Foundation
• Nearly 2,100 employees serve more than 14,000 students100 percent of students receive free lunch
• Home to San Antonio's first STEM Early College High School. STEM Early College High School gives students the opportunity to earn up to 60 hours of college credit and an associate degree before they even graduate high school
• Offering dual language classes
• Offering an array of educational, physical, artistic, and social extracurricular activities
• Texas 21st Century ACE grant recipient
• Dual Credit program allows students to earn college credit while still in high school
• Career & Technology Education courses provide students with the skills necessary to enter a post-secondary education or career.

DISTRICT STORY

Harlandale Independent School District is nestled in the southside of San Antonio, where history and traditions thrive. We take pride in honoring our unique cultural heritage, while delivering a high-quality educational experience. What began as a one-room schoolhouse in a granary a Mission San Jose in 1894, is now a multi-campus urban school district.

HISD comprises 20 traditional campuses, an early college high school, an alternative educational school, a campus dedicated to children with extensive disabilities and a center for early childhood education. With a 98 percent Hispanic population, our hearts beat in two languages. HISD offers a dual language program at the elementary and middle school level. Middle school students can take pre-advanced placement classes. At the high school level, students can take advanced placement classes, dual credit, and a multitude of career & technology courses.

DEMOGRAPHICS

Student Enrollment: 14,377 Students

Student Demographics:
• African American: 0.3%
• Asian: 0.1%
• Hispanic: 97.9%
• Native American: 0%
• Pacific Islander: 0%
• White: 1.6%
• Two or more races: 0.1%
• Economically Disadvantaged: 87.3%

Number of Schools: 23
Total Employees: 2,142
Student/Teacher Ratio: 14.3
Average Student Expenditure: $10,727

HOW TO REACH US

102 Genevieve, San Antonio, Texas 78214-2997

210-989-4300
www.harlandale.net

Twitter: @HarlandaleISD
Facebook: @HarlandaleFamily
Instagram: @HarlandaleISD
YouTube: HarlandaleISDSATX

JUDSON ISD, est. 1958

JUDSON INDEPENDENT SCHOOL DISTRICT

District Mission
All Judson ISD students will receive a quality education enabling them to become successful in a global society.

District Highlights
• Accountability Rating Letter Grade: B
• Holdsworth Center Partner in Leadership Development
• All day Pre-K for children 3 and 4 years of age at all elementary schools
• School of Choice District (Regardless of resident location)
• More Than 30 Career Certifications for The Workplace
• Robust STEM programs from elementary through high School

Our Beliefs
• Judson ISD believes in an equitable education that looks beyond academic scores; students feel empowered and capable of developing their identity, dreams, and goals
• Judson ISD believes in creating a culture of service that places respect, honesty, open communication, innovation, and collaboration at the forefront to create a safe sense of community and lifelong learners
• Judson ISD believes that positive relationships among students, staff, families, and community members make them feel valued, safe, and trusted so they will be involved and empowered to make informed decisions about the future of our district and students

Our Promise to Students, All students will:
• Receive an equitable education in a safe learning environment
• Meet or exceed grade level expectations
• Graduate college, career or military ready
• Be inspired to discover and develop their unique abilities, talents, and voice

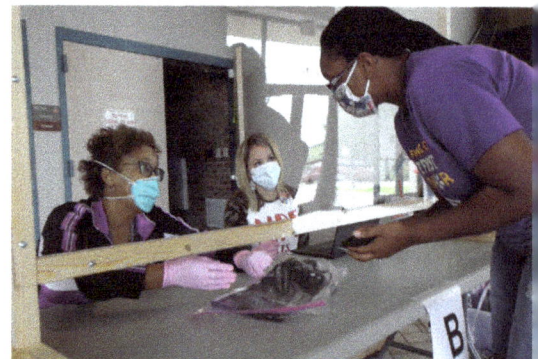

DISTRICT STORY

Judson Independent School District is in northeast Bexar County, uniquely serving the community by our geographic location. We serve seven different municipalities, including Schertz, Selma, Converse, Live Oak, Universal City, San Antonio, and Kirby.

On June 25, 1958, the Bexar County School Board formed the Rural High School District No. 8 by combining the school districts at that time of Converse, Kirby, and Selma to better serve the area. In December of 1966, voters elected to form the Judson Independent School District named after Moses Judson, a strong advocate for education.

Judson has grown from 432 students in the beginning to now more than 22,000. We are one of the most ethnically diverse school districts in San Antonio and the state. Judson has grown from 432 students in the beginning to now more than 22,000. Our district boundaries cover almost 56 square miles, across 7 cities, comprising 33 campuses. Our district includes a stand-alone, nationally ranked, early college campus and an early childhood focus. Our early childhood program serves families with a dynamic all-day Pre-K program at each elementary campus.

DEMOGRAPHICS

Student Enrollment: 22,848 Students

Student Demographics:
· African American: 21.4%
· Asian: 2.0%
· Hispanic: 57.1%
· Native American: 0.3%
· Pacific Islander: 0.3%
· White: 14.8%
· Two or more races: 3.7%
· Economically Disadvantaged: 67.5%

Number of Schools: 32
Total Employees: 3,370
Student/Teacher Ratio: 14.2
Avg Student Expenditure: $9,324

HOW TO REACH US

Judson ISD 8012 Shin Oak, Live Oak Texas 78233

210-945-5100
www.judsonisd.org

Google Play Store: JISD Connect
Facebook: @judsonisd
Twitter: @judsonisd
Instagram: @judsonisd_official
YouTube: judsonisdtv

LACKLAND ISD, est. 1953

LACKLAND
Independent School District

District Mission
Lackland ISD empowers students to construct successful futures.

District Beliefs
• We believe in creating and facilitating opportunities to expand and utilize essential skills for all
• That all students deserve equal access to individual opportunities
• Everyone benefits when they question to understand "why" ideas are relevant
• Education is a shared partnership
• In effective communication in a respectful environment

District Highlights
• Serves over 96% military-connected students
• Provides One to One I-Pad program for PK - 12th grade
• HEB Excellence in Education Award for Best Small School District
• Provides the Elementary Success for All (SFA) Reading Program
• Promotes the Jr. & Sr. High Robotics Programs
• Recognizes a 100% graduation rate (18-19)
• Partners with Northside ISD's John Jay HS for JROTC
• Provides free breakfast for all students
• Consistently performs at high levels on the Texas Accountability System
• Ensures robust special programs and supports for English Language Learners, Gifted and Talented, Career and Technology Education, Special Education, State Compensatory Education and Dyslexia

District Vision
The Premier leader in educational excellence.

DISTRICT STORY

The beginnings of Lackland ISD are closely connected to those of Lackland Air Force Base. The base was established on June 26, 1942, after the War Department separated part of Kelly Field and named it the San Antonio Aviation Cadet Center (SAACC). In 1947, Lackland Air Force Base was created and was named for Brigadier General Frank D. Lackland, former Kelly Field Commander. The Bexar County Judges approved the establishment of Lackland ISD. With a desire to provide on-site education for the children of military personnel, Lackland AFB officials petitioned the Health, Education, and Welfare Department in 1951 for school building funds. The Texas Education Agency (TEA) was also petitioned to establish an accredited school district. In 1953, TEA and the office of the Bexar County Judge approved the establishment of Lackland ISD.

Lackland ISD opened its doors to students in grades 1-6 on September 8, 1953. During the 1950s and 1960s, junior and high school age students attended schools in the San Antonio ISD. In 1967, secondary classrooms and a gymnasium (now our elementary gymnasium) were completed for grades beyond 6th grade. One grade level was added a year, beginning with the 7th grade in 1968-1969.

DEMOGRAPHICS

Student Enrollment: 1,072 Students

Student Demographics:
• African American: 12.4%
• Hispanic: 24.9%
• White: 45.99%
• Asian: 1.87
• Pacific Islander: 1.03%
• Two /More Races: 13.8%
• Economically Disadvantaged: 24.16%

Number of Schools: 2
Total Employees: 190
Student/Teacher Ratio: 12.1
Expenditure: $14,187

HOW TO REACH US

2460 Kenly Ave Building 8265, San Antonio, Texas 78236

210-357-5000
www.lacklandisd.net

Twitter: @lisdtx
Facebook: @lisdtx

MEDINA VALLEY
INDEPENDENT SCHOOL DISTRICT

District Mission

MVISD will provide its students with a superior and diverse

education that inspires excellence, promotes accountability and values, and encourages all students to achieve their highest potential.

District Highlights

- Accountability
- TEA District Rating = A (2018 & 2019)
- TASA Honor Board (2018)
- 2019 TEA Campus Distinction Designations = (28): in math, science, English/Language Arts, social studies, academic growth, closing the gaps, postsecondary readiness (District postsecondary readiness included)
- MVHS named to the Texas Honor Roll 2019 Graduates
- Graduation Rate = 98.9%
- Graduates earning Foundation High School Program with Endorsement or Distinguished Level Achievement = 96.3%
- Dual Credit
- 5012 free college hours earned in 2019 (Value = $826,469)
- Dual Credit courses (17 course titles; 49 college hours offered)
- Articulated College Courses (6)
- Industry Based Certifications - 216 earned (2018-19)
- FFA Program (26+ Extracurricular Programs)
- Supervised Agricultural Experience (SAE) Leadership Development Events (LDE)
- Career Development Events (CDE) Speaking Development Events (SDE)

District Vision

Our community will engage students and adults in a challenging educational environment that inspires creativity and enriches lives for today's realities and tomorrow's possibilities. Engage. Inspire. Enrich.

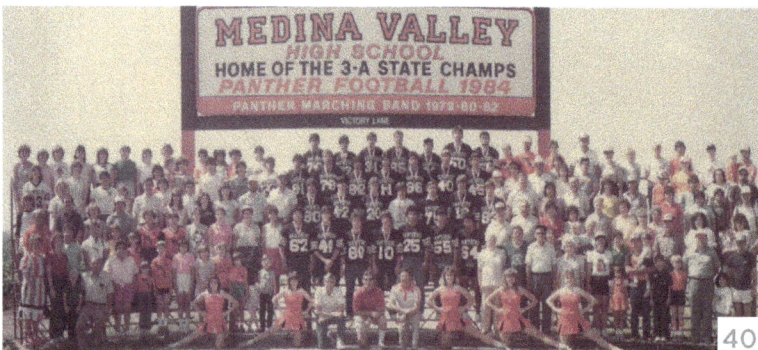

District Goals
- Continue and expand focus on safety including: expansion of camera coverage, exterior and classroom door safety, and increase number of SRO's
- Continue focus on curriculum, including closing achievement gaps, use of technology in the classroom, development of an 18+ program in special education, continued expansion of CTE and dual credit, and consistency of programs across campuses

DISTRICT STORY

Medina Valley ISD encompasses 300 square miles and is located west of San Antonio. The proud students of the Panther Nation come from Castroville, La Coste, Rio Medina, Dunlay, Mico, parts of San Antonio and surrounding areas. The district has approximately 5,500 students with 7 campuses (4 elementary, 2 middle schools, and 1 high school). Medina Valley ISD is one of the fastest growing districts in the state.

History Facts
Medina Valley ISD was formed in 1960 with the consolidation of the La Coste and Castroville schools. At the time of consolidation, an estimated 550 students were enrolled in the district. Today, the district has an estimated 5,500 students - ten times the amount at consolidation. The original elementary school currently serves as Castroville City Hall. MVISD is the fastest growing school district in ESC Region 20 and the second in ESC Region13. Growth is seen in a 7-10% increase in student enrollment every year. The district consistently outscores all State averages in accountability ratings and testing, producing well-round- ed career -minded students. The -district recently received an "A" rating from the Texas Education Agency.

DEMOGRAPHICS

Student Enrollment: 6,100 Students

Student Demographics:
- African American: 3.5 %
- Asian: 0.6%
- Hispanic: 58.2%
- Native American: 0.6%
- Pacific Islander: 0.2%
- White: 34.3%
- Two or more races: 2.7%
- Economically Disadvantaged: 52.1%

Number of Schools: 7
Total Employees: 620
Student/Teacher Ratio: 17.5
Avg Student Expenditure: $8,561

HOW TO REACH US

8449 FM 471 South Castroville, Texas 78009

830-931-2243
www.mvisd.com
mvisdnotify@mvisd.org

iTunes App: MVISD
Twitter: @medinavalleyisd
Facebook: @medinavalleyschools
Instagram: @MEDINAVALLEY

NORTH EAST ISD, est. 1950

District Highlights

North East ISD is home to approximately 64,000 students and 9,000 employees, of whom 4,300 are teachers. Our campuses include 46 elementary schools, 14 middle schools, 7 high schools, 1 magnet school and 12 magnet programs. Our Career and Technical Education Center offers student programs in health professions; diesel and automotive technology; and construction trades, including electrical, welding. HVAC, and plumbing. This is in addition to the countless other career and technical courses offered at all our high schools. North East ISD offers multiple dual credit and Advanced Placement (AP) course opportunities. In 2018, more than 33,000 college credit hours were earned by NEISD students. NEISD opened its first dedicated full-day Pre-K Academy in fall 2019. The Academy features Science, Technology, Engineering, Art, and Math (STEAM) focused curriculum and dual language classrooms. It will also offer enrichment, such as music, physical education, and library services.

District Mission

We challenge and encourage each student to achieve and demonstrate academic excellence, technical skills, and responsible citizenship.

Goals

• Will prepare our students for college and workforce readiness by challenging them to maximize their knowledge, technological skills, and potential for learning through both academic achievement and personal excellence.

• Will provide and maintain safe, supportive, and equitable learning environments for our students

• Will ensure campuses serve as centers for community involvement.

• Will develop and promote positive relationships through communication, involvement, and partnerships with our community.

• Will continue to use best practices in its efficient and effective.

DISTRICT STORY

North East ISD was established in 1950. Today, it is the second-largest school district in San Antonio. North East ISD has a long-standing history of success in academics and extracurricular activities. Our students exhibit great leadership in and out of the classroom. Our teachers are recognized at the local, state, and national level for their expertise and contributions to the field of education. We set the standard high for our employees because we want to provide the best for our students.

Educator Excellence
• North East ISD teachers, on average, have 12 years of teaching experience and are among the highest paid in Texas.
• Forbes ranked North East ISD as one of America's Best Employers in 2018.
• Each year, North East ISD teachers mentor approximately 250 student teachers working toward their degree in education.
• North East ISD and the Tobin Center for the Performing Arts partner with the Kennedy Center to expand the District's use of art integration in classrooms. North East ISD teachers embrace technology integration in the classroom from Pre-K through high school graduation.

DEMOGRAPHICS

Student Enrollment: 60,483 Students

Student Demographics:
• African American: 7.35%
• Asian: 3.9%
• Hispanic: 60.5%
• Native American: 0.26%
• Pacific Islander: 0.1%
• White: 23.92%
• Two or more races: 3.91%
• Economically Disadvantaged: 46.4%

Number of Schools: 75
Total Employees: 8,831
Student/Teacher Ratio: 15.3
Avg Student Expenditure: $9,195

HOW TO REACH US

8961 Tesoro Dr., San Antonio, Texas 78217

210-407-0000
www.neisd.net

Twitter: @NEISD
Facebook: @NorthEastISD
Instagram: @northeastisd
YouTube: NorthEastISD

NORTHSIDE ISD, est. 1949

District Mission
Transform the Learning Experience for Students.

District Motto
San Antonio's Premier School District of Choice.

District Highlights
Passionate & Dedicated Staff
Northside ISD fosters an environment where highly qualified Educators inspire and motivate students. In addition to our Certified teachers, our amazing support staff in critical Departments like child nutrition, transportation, counseling, custodial & maintenance, and health services come together for the success of our students.

Future Ready Leaders
We lay the foundation for students to succeed in college, career, or the military. Northside ISD offers programs from innovative Career & Technical Education (CTE) and Advancement Via Individual Determination (AVID) which is designed to help underachieving students with high academic potential prepare for entrance to colleges and universities.

Challenging Academics
We offer a variety of academic programs designed to engage all students, including nine specialized magnet programs. Among others, these programs include full and half-day Pre-K, Gifted & Talented, dual credit, STEM/STEAM, and advanced placement. For continuous learning after the school day has ended, we offer the Learning Tree after-school enrichment program at the elementary and middle school levels.

Diverse Population
We recognize all students' individualized needs in an inclusive and supporting environment. Our special education, bilingual and dual-language, and gifted & talented programs offer a small glimpse into that effort.

DISTRICT STORY

Established in 1949 by the consolidation of 12 rural school districts, Northside Independent School District (NISD) today is 355 square miles of urban landscape, suburban communities, and rural Texas hill country. NISD is home to more than 102,700 students in 124 schools. In addition to traditional K-12 schools, we offer specialized magnet programs in seven high schools and two middle schools.

You Belong in Northside ISD
We believe every student deserves the highest quality education and it is our mission to transform their learning experience. We know a key to student success includes dedicated, passionate teachers engaging with students. Teachers who provide each student the opportunity to create and learn in new and exciting ways. We know that relationships between students and their families, educators, and the community are vital to their success. These supportive dynamics help each student find their voice so they can contribute and engage in their communities now and in the future.

District Vision:
Every day, every student grows in confidence, curiosity, and capability.

DEMOGRAPHICS

Student Enrollment: 102,700 Students

Student Demographics:
• African American: 6.6%
• Asian: 3.3%
• Hispanic: 68.1%
• Native American: 0.1%
• Pacific Islander: 0.2%
• White: 18.1%
• Two or more races: 3.4%
• Economically Disadvantaged: 47.9%

Number of Schools: 124
Total Employees: 13,484
Student/Teacher Ratio: 15.3
Avg Student Expenditure: $8,814

HOW TO REACH US

5900 Evers Road, San Antonio, Texas 78238

210-397-8500
info@nisd.net
www.nisd.net

Twitter: @NISD
Facebook: @NorthsideISD
Instagram: @northsideisd
Youtube: @northsideisd

RANDOLPH FIELD ISD, est. 1933

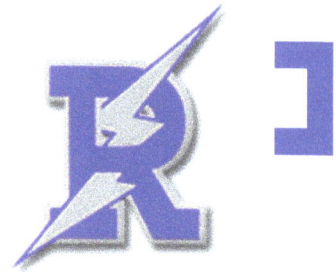

District Mission

Randolph Field ISD prepares students to be life-long learners who are successful, productive, and responsible citizens. To achieve this purpose, students will access and process information, solve problems, and communicate. Utilizing technology to facilitate their learning, students will learn and work as individuals as well as within teams.

District Highlights

• The Randolph Elementary School and the Randolph Middle School have both been designated National Blue-Ribbon Schools by the U. S. Department of Education

• Diverse core curriculum including dual credit and advanced placement courses. Our motto, "Dedicated to excellence," is evidenced in our commitment to ensuring our students achieve at high levels

• Annual campus goals focus on increased numbers of students achieving at the advanced academic level on state assessments rather than simply on meeting minimum standards

• Challenging curriculum provides a deeper understanding of learning, and the rigor of our programs is constantly reviewed and revised to continually extend our students' learning

• Extraordinary extracurricular activities which include a UIL Top 10-rated band and an award-winning art program

• Fine arts program also extends to our elementary campus with art, music, and foreign language

• Seniors annually receive more than $1 million in academic scholarships

• Awarded over $6 million in Department of Defense Education Activity grants to support both academic achievement and social-emotional well-being for our military children

DISTRICT STORY

Randolph Field Independent School District is located on Joint Base San Antonio in Universal City, Texas, and has proudly served military families for more than sixty years. Randolph Elementary School's song says it well: "Our parents serve the nation; our school reflects the best." Among the U. S. military, our district enjoys an excellent reputation for meeting the academic and social-emotional needs of children. Military-connected families trust RFISD, as more than 65% of our students choose our schools even though they live in other school districts, often quite a distance away. Our district under-stands the unique pressures and demands faced by today's military families, and we consistently go the extra mile to support our students and families.

Randolph Field Independent School District, often ranked as the number one district in the greater San Antonio area, consistently exceeds state and federal accountability standards and remains committed to excellence. As of September 28, 2018 (Impact Aid survey data), we had 1,467 students of whom 80.81% are from active duty or retired military personnel.

DEMOGRAPHICS

Student Enrollment: 1,467 Students

Student Demographics:
• African American: 17.1%
• Asian: 3.5%
• Hispanic: 22.6%
• Native American: 0%
• Pacific Islander: 1.2%
• White: 44.6%
• Two or more races: 11%
• Economically Disadvantaged: 7.9%

Number of Schools: 3
Total Employees: 199
Student/Teacher Ratio: 14.3
Avg Student Expenditure: $11,239

HOW TO REACH US

Post Office Box 2217 Universal City, Texas 78148-1214

210-357-2300

Twitter: @RandolphRoHawks
Facebook: Randolph Field ISD

SAN ANTONIO ISD, est. 1903

District Mission
To transform SAISD into a national model urban school district where every child graduates and is educated so that he or she is prepared to be a contributing member of the community.

District Vision
Our primary purpose of improving lives through a quality education is driven by an unrelenting determination to graduate all our students and prepare them for success in higher education. Our ideology is reflected in our fundamental beliefs, commitments and core values that guide us in our daily practices.

District Highlights
• Three early college high schools, as well as magnet programs and dual-credit opportunities in every comprehensive high school
• 50 schools with dual language programs
• Nine schools with the International Baccalaureate (IB) framework: Six IB World schools and three IB Candidate schools. The only district in the county with IB at the elementary, middle, and high school levels
• 79% of SAISD students participate in fine arts
• All K-5 students are provided with art class
• The $1.3 billion Bond 2020 and the $450 million Bond 2016 are funding technology enhancements, security upgrades, school renovations, and creating 21st-century learning environments
• Investments in technology in every school include more than $7 million in grant funding for a high-speed fiber network to bring fast and reliable connectivity into the classroom
• Every school bus has Wi-Fi to provide riders with access to homework resources and the BiblioTech audiobook library
• Partnership with the Culinary Institute of America has produced new recipes and provided training for all Child Nutrition employees

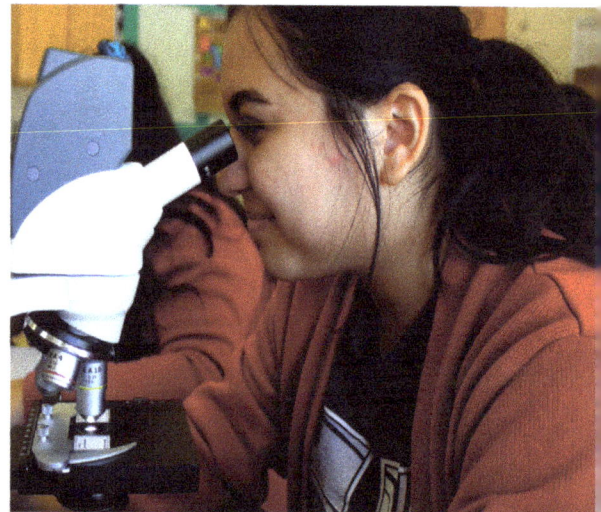

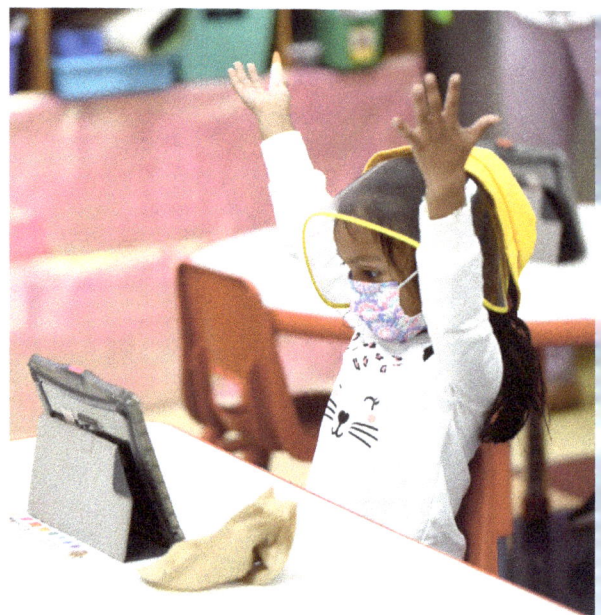

DISTRICT STORY

The San Antonio Independent School District is as diverse and historically rich as the city whose name it shares. As San Antonio's founding school district, SAISD neighborhood schools have served as the heart of San Antonio for more than 100 years.

Today, SAISD serves about 46,000 students across almost 100 schools in our culturally proud, urban community. True to our roots, SAISD continues to pave the way in San Antonio with the city's only public Montessori school, single-gender campuses, and K-12 International Baccalaureate framework. We also have the largest number of campuses offering a dual language education. SAISD students can customize their own educational experience and find what truly drives them through the city's academic programs and specialized schools. Every student has a journey, and SAISD is supporting that path wherever it may lead for each of its students. From extensive athletics to fine arts, including a mariachi curriculum that was pioneered right here in our District before being modeled across the nation, the spirit of SAISD can be found in the traditional classroom, programs, and activities.

Core Values
- Student-centered
- High expectations
- Commitment
- Passion
- Integrity
- Respect
- Teamwork

DEMOGRAPHICS

Student Enrollment: 45,921 Students

Student Demographics:
- African American: 6.04%
- Asian: 0.44%
- Hispanic: 89.92%
- Native American: 0.12%
- Pacific Islander: 0.03%
- White: 2.83%
- Two or more races: 0.63%
- Economically Disadvantaged: 87.43%

Number of Schools: 99
Total Employees: 7,531 FTE
Student/Teacher Ratio: 15.6
Average Student Expenditure: $9,798

HOW TO REACH US

141 Lavaca Street San Antonio, Texas 78210

210-554-2200
www.saisd.net

Twitter: @SAISD
Facebook: @SanAntonioISD
Instagram: @SanAntonioISD
YouTube: @SAISDCommunications

SCUC ISD "A District with Passion and Purpose!"

District Mission
SCUC ISD, a diverse community founded in trust and transparency, commits to empower all students to fulfill lifelong potential through inspiring learning experiences.

District Values
- Leadership
- Character
- Commitment
- Service
- Learning

Vision
Inspire – Innovate – EXCEL!

Values
Leadership, Character, Commitment, Service, Learning

District Highlights
- One of the highest completion rates in the state at 98%
- 82% of Class of 2020 graduates were certified in a combination of college credits, career certifications, military enlistment, and/or appointment to one of the nation's service academies
- Selected for the Top Workplace Award by the San Antonio Express News for seven consecutive years and eight out of the last ten years
- Received a Superior Rating for the 17th consecutive year by the Financial Integrity Rating System of Texas
- 85% or more of its secondary-level students (grades 7-12) participate in high-quality extra-curricular activities
- Rated as a Best Communities for Music Education designation from The NAMM Foundation for its outstanding commitment to music education for two consecutive years
- Samuel Clemens High School Cheer captured the Class 6A Division II UIL State Championship

DISTRICT STORY

Area schools began in 1877 as the Lower Valley School (closed in 1966) and the Green Valley School (closed in 1955). School districts of Schertz and Cibolo merged in 1940.

SCUC is comprised of eight elementary schools, three intermediate campuses, two junior high schools, two traditional high schools, an at-risk high school, a disciplinary education program, and an 18+ Transition Program. Nearly 37 percent of the student enrollment is comprised of military-related families.

The SCUC ISD Education Foundation has donated over $324,000 to District schools since its inception in 2008 to fund Innovative Teacher Grants.

DEMOGRAPHICS

Student Enrollment: 15,649 Students

Student Demographics:
· African American: 11.58%
· Asian/Pacific Islander: 1.85%
· Hispanic: 44.63%
· Native American: 0.33%
· White: 34.4%
· Two or more races: 6.91%
· Economically Disadvantaged: 28.3

Number of Schools: 17
Total Employees: 1,977
Student/Teacher Ratio: 16.7
Teachers: 1,016
Avg Student Expenditure: $8,099

HOW TO REACH US

1060 Elbel Road, Schertz, Texas 78154

210-945-6200
www.scuc.txed.net

Twitter: @SCUCISD
Facebook: @scucisd
Instagram: @scucisd
YouTube: @SCUCISD

SOMERSET, est. 1922

District Mission
The mission of the Somerset Independent School District is to provide exemplary preparation for higher education and life.

District Core Values
We believe that "Hard Work Pays Off" and every graduate will be college, career, and citizenship ready. In 2019, Somerset ISD earned an overall district accountability grade of "87" from the TEA, one of the highest scores for any school district in our area.

District Highlights:
- 2020 National Award for Excellence for Educator Effectiveness
- 2016 Texas Board of the Year – H.E.B. Excellence in Education Award
- National Institute for Excellence in Teaching Founder's Award Finalists – 3 Years
- Ranked in the Top Quartile in Academics Among Bexar County Districts
- A+ Superior Rating
- Texas Milken Educator Teacher Award
- ESC-20 Secondary Teacher of the Year
- Statewide GEAR UP Principal of the Year
- One-to-One Technology Initiative
- K-12 STEM Curriculum
- Skills USA National Champions
- Elementary-Secondary Robotics, Fembots, and Aquabots
- Google Certified Teachers Grades 3 – High School
- 100% Early College High School Graduation Rate – Associate's Degree
- Head Start Partnership Program
- Toyota U.S.A. Foundation Award - $200,000
- San Antonio Area Foundation Award - $50,000
- Robust Career and Technical Education Industry Offerings and Certifications
- State-Ranked ROTC
- Alamo Promise and Jaguar Achiever Promise

DISTRICT STORY

Somerset ISD occupies 85 square miles encompassing students from the cities of Somerset, Atascosa, Poteet, Von Ormy, San Antonio, and surrounding rural areas. SISD has seven campuses serving students from Pre-Kindergarten through twelfth grade. In recent years, SISD has experienced growth in student population reflective of the general population growth in Southern Bexar County.

The success of Somerset ISD is rooted in bold and innovative leadership decisions that advance all aspects of the system. In the last few years, Somerset has become a frontrunner with teaching, learning, and leading. "One team, one voice" is the district's mantra for leadership, as it precisely communicates a unified team approach to leadership with consistent messaging about our mission and focus: students. There are high levels of account-ability for individual and team outcomes, and every decision is based on what is right for students.

Leaders in Somerset ISD understand that their primary purpose is to serve the constit-uents: students, parents, teachers, and our community in a way that ensures collective direction and unity when taking action. We assume a 360-degree approach to leading that mobilizes, influences, and guides others towards desired experiences, beliefs, actions, and results.

District Beliefs
"Ever since I can remember, I knew I wanted to be a teacher. I always want my kids to do it their way. Show me what you have and show me something different."

DEMOGRAPHICS

Student Enrollment: 4,024 Students

Student Demographics:
• American Indian/Alaskan: 0.2%
• Asian: 0.4%
• African American: 0.27%
• Hispanic: 92.02%
• White: 6.83%
• Hawaiian/Pacific Islander: 0.5%
• Two or More Races: 0.70%
• Economically Disadvantaged: 77.2%

Number of Schools: 7
Total Employees: 597
Student/Teacher Ratio: 15.5
Average Student Expenditure: $10,378

HOW TO REACH US

7791 6th Street, P.O. BOX 279, Somerset, Texas 78069

210-750-8955
www.sisdk12.edlioschool.com

Twitter: @somersetisd
Facebook: @SomersetISDBulldogs

SOUTH SAN ISD, est. 1922

District Mission
All students enjoy successful education experiences, empowering them to make decisions while enriching their lives in the future they create.

District Beliefs
• We believe in constructive engagement of the school community for the success of our district
• We believe in a strong support system for the school community to achieve excellence
• We believe that innovative and challenging experiences for all students produce successful learners
• We believe that trusting relationships among the school community are essential to student success
• We believe that an inclusive school culture promotes positive student development and voice
• We believe strong and effective student and adult leadership is essential to build a culture of high expectations

District Highlights
• Class of 2020 awarded $9,826,077 in scholarships
• Class of 2020 earned 6,000 hours in college credits
• Nearly 1,400 employees serve more than 8,700 students
• Awarded 7-year GEAR UP Grant in partnership with UTIPSI
• Awarded TEA's Community Partnership Grant
• Two elementary campuses nominated two years in a row for a Capturing Kids Heart Award
• High School students enrolled in the Health Science Academy will gain the knowledge and skills for a successful career in Health Science Fields such as EMT, Pharmacy Tech, and LVN
• Early College High School gives students the opportunity to earn up to 60 hours of college credit and an associate degree
• 22 Career and Technical Education Pathways equipping students with the skills they need for 21st-century professions
• Middle School Choice Academies: Fine Arts Academy, Health Science Academy, STEM Academy and Architecture, Construction, and Design
• Designated Elementary Bilingual Clusters
• Provide after-school childcare
• Head Start Program is offered at all elementary schools
• 100% of students receive free lunch management of District resources.
• Will foster a culture of health and wellness among our students, staff, and community.

DISTRICT STORY

The South San Antonio Independent School District is in the well-established south and southwest portion of San Antonio, covering 21 square miles. South San ISD provides outstanding instructional programs for Pre-K through grade twelve. The faculty and support staff are committed to providing innovative and challenging experiences to produce successful learners.

South San ISD offers four Middle School Choice Academies with open enrollment available to all Bexar County middle school students. Students at all four Choice Academies will benefit from AVID, project-based learning, Pre-AP Courses, and high school credit courses.

South San Antonio High School students can enroll in several programs to include Early College, Dual Credit, Advanced Placement, Health Science Academy, and more than 22 Career and Technical Education pathways.

DEMOGRAPHICS

Student Enrollment: 8,300 Students

Student Demographics:
• African American: 1.1%
• Asian: 0.1%
• Hispanic: 97.2%
• Native American: 0.1%
• Pacific Islander: 0.1%
• White: 1.3%
• Two or more races: 0.1%
• Economically Disadvantaged: 86.5%

Number of Schools: 16
Total Employees: 1,279
Student/Teacher Ratio: 16.4
Avg Student Expenditure: $11,054

HOW TO REACH US

1450 Gillette Blvd. San Antonio, Texas 78224

210-977-7000
www.southsanisd.net

Twitter: @SSAISD
Facebook: @southsanantonioisd
Instagram: @southsanisd
YouTube: SouthSanAntonio

SOUTHSIDE ISD, est. 1913

District Mission
Southside ISD seeks to be the choice when it comes to providing a quality public education by upholding the highest standards of our core values. Our core values and high standards drive Southside ISD's quality education and serve as a preferred choice for students.

District Highlights
• Menchaca Early Childhood Center is a nationally recognized Pre-K and Kindergarten state of the art facility for early childhood education.
• Freedom Elementary is A Two-way Dual Language and Leader in Me School. We sow the 7 habits today to grow leaders for tomorrow by living our mission and vision to be the best that we can be!
• Graduated 36 students in 2019 with an associate degree from Palo Alto College
• Southside ISD Education Foundation raised more than $77,000 in 2019.
• District of Innovation
• PBIS (Positive Behavior Interventions and Support) district and has initiatives focused on Behavioral Health

Programs:
• 1:1 Technology Blended Learning
• Early Childhood Education Head Start
• Gifted and Talented
• Kinesthetic/Physical Learning
• Social Emotional Learning

Every student
• College and Career-Ready

District Core Values
• Service. Accountability. Integrity. Loyalty.

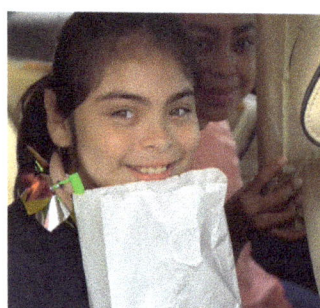

DISTRICT STORY

Southside Independent School District is a public-school district located in southern Bexar County, Texas. It serves the far south side of San Antonio, Texas. Southside ISD was created to address the physical and intellectual needs of a growing student population in the Southside community. Southside ISD consists of 8 schools serving more than 5,800 students and 920 employees and approximately 380 teachers. Southside ISD has a Board of Managers.

Philanthropist Kym Rapier gifted $1.5 Million to Southside ISD to provide health treatment to students, teachers, and families at the school district's Susan Hall Community Health Clinic which opened in May 2019. The clinic will offer laboratory services, X-Rays, and COVID-19 testing. The clinic is named in honor of Ms. Rapier's late mother, Susan Hall.

Did-you-know information about Southside ISD:
- Teachers rank #1 in teacher pay in the area
- 145 high school seniors received scholarships last year totaling more than two-million dollars
- Parents never have to pay a penny for their children's meals at southside ISD. All children qualify for free breakfast, lunch, and supper
- High school students earned more than 120 industry-based certifications last year in programs like health science, graphic design, welding, electrical technology
- All high school seniors receive the Alamo promise a two-year grant to any of the Alamo colleges
- Families can receive help with food. Thanks to our partnership with the San Antonio Food Bank
- Principals have been nominated for the prestigious HEB excellence in education award
- 36 seniors earned their college associates degrees last year
- Bus drivers are the highest paid bus drivers in the area
- Served nearly three-quarters of a million lunches to our students last year

DEMOGRAPHICS

Student Enrollment: 5,607 Students

Student Demographics:
- African American: 1.6 %
- Asian: 0.2%
- Hispanic: 90.9%
- Native American: 0%
- Pacific Islander: 0%
- White: 7%
- Two or more races: 0.4%
- Economically Disadvantaged: 82.1%

Number of Schools: 8
Total Employees: 920
Student/Teacher Ratio: 15.2
Average Student Expenditure: $10,779

HOW TO REACH US

1460 Martinez Losoya Rd, San Antonio, Texas 78221

210-882-1600
www.southsideisd.org

Facebook: @southsideisd
Twitter: @Southsideisd

SOUTHWEST ISD, est. 1951

District Beliefs
- Instruction: SWISD will provide a comprehensive framework of learning that is engaging, flexible, rigorous, supportive, and relevant to college/career readiness for all students
- Social/Emotional Environment: SWISD will foster an environment in which social and emotional support is a priority for all
- Communication: SWISD will consistently utilize timely, multifaceted communications reaching all members of our SWISD community
- Academic Environment: SWISD will create safe, nurturing, and engaging environment where all learners succeed
- Community Engagement: SWISD will capitalize on the strengths, resources, and abilities of our diverse community to support students in becoming successful, global citizens
- Professional Development: SWISD will provide relevant professional development to meet the needs of all learners in a timely manner

District Highlights
- Free, all-day Pre-K for the SWISD community
- Paid internship programs with HOLT CAT, Joeris General Contractors, and Toyota Motor Manufacturing, Texas
- One of seven districts selected for the inaugural class of Holdsworth leadership training
- Host annual SWISD Olympic Fiesta, an official FIESTA event for the community
- SW High School Band and Orchestra invited to perform at Carnegie Hall in New York City (2015)
- SW High School Engineering Team invited to White House to meet President Barack Obama (2014)
- SWISD School Board selected as Region 20 School Board of the Year and the Texas-E-B School Board of the Year Finalist (2017-18)
- SWISD Superintendent of the Year, Region 20, Recipient (2019)
- Superior rating from the Financial Integrity Rating System of Texas and a Gold Star Status from the Comptroller's Leadership Award for Financial Transparency

DISTRICT STORY

We are Southwest!
Southwest Independent School District (SWISD) was established in 1951 when five rural districts, covering 115 square miles of rural and urban areas, merged. SWISD is the sixth-largest school district in Bexar County, serving almost 14,000 students. One of seven districts selected for the inaugural class of Holdsworth leadership training, SWISD prides itself in its family friendly Schools. SWISD consists of 11 elementary schools, 4 middle schools, and 3 high schools which include CAST STEM, an in-district charter focused on engineering, energy, technology, and advanced manufacturing. From robotics to aviation, SWISD offers educational opportunities at all grade levels. SWISD offers dual credit courses, advanced placement classes, and several career and technology pathways, including paid internships with industry partners.

District Mission
Southwest Independent School District will identify and develop the potential of all individuals.

DEMOGRAPHICS

Student Enrollment: 13,773 Students

Student Demographics:
• African American - 3. 1%
• Asian - .4%
• Hispanic - 90.4%
• Native American - 0.2%
• Pacific Islander - 0.1%
• White – 5.2%
• Two or more races - 0.8%
• Economically Disadvantaged: 85.1%

Number of schools: 19
Total employees: 1,873
Student/Teacher Ratio: 15.5
Avg Student Expenditure: $11,190

HOW TO REACH US

11914 Dragon Lane San Antonio, Texas 78252

210-622-4300
www.swisd.net

Twitter: @SWISD
Facebook: @SWISDsatx
Instagram: @southwestisd
YouTube: swisdtv

CHAPTER THREE

BEXAR COUNTY ISDs AND COVID-19
THE FIRST 60 DAYS

BEXAR COUNTY ISDs AND COVID-19
The First 60 Days

For Texas, the impact of COVID-19 began on February 7, 2020 when the U.S. Department of Health and Human Services began transporting American citizens evacuated from the Hubei province of China to Joint Base San Antonio-Lackland Air Force base. They were diverted to Lackland AFB because of possible exposure to COVID-19. On February 13, 2020, the first documented case in Texas was confirmed among those that were evacuated. Shortly thereafter, San Antonio and Bexar County declared a local state disaster and public health emergency. Although there was no community spread from that case, the city and surrounding area went on high alert. Two days later a positive case was reported in Fort Bend County. This case was the first case in Texas reported external to the Lackland quarantine group. In a rapidly evolving situation, cases were soon reported in other areas of Texas. (14)

On March 13, Governor Greg Abbott issued a statewide disaster proclamation certifying that COVID-19 posed an imminent threat of danger. In March, he issued Executive Orders that closed schools to in-person classroom attendance for the school year. (15) During that time, the San Antonio area ISDs were either on spring break or returning from it. Most of the ISDs made the decision not to return to campus. When the ISDs received news of the Governor's orders, they immediately took action to ensure that the services necessary for the students and their families continued while students did not have access to the campuses. These vital services provided for the mental, physiological, and emotional needs of students and families. These services included:

- School meals
- Distance learning
- Counseling
- Community engagement

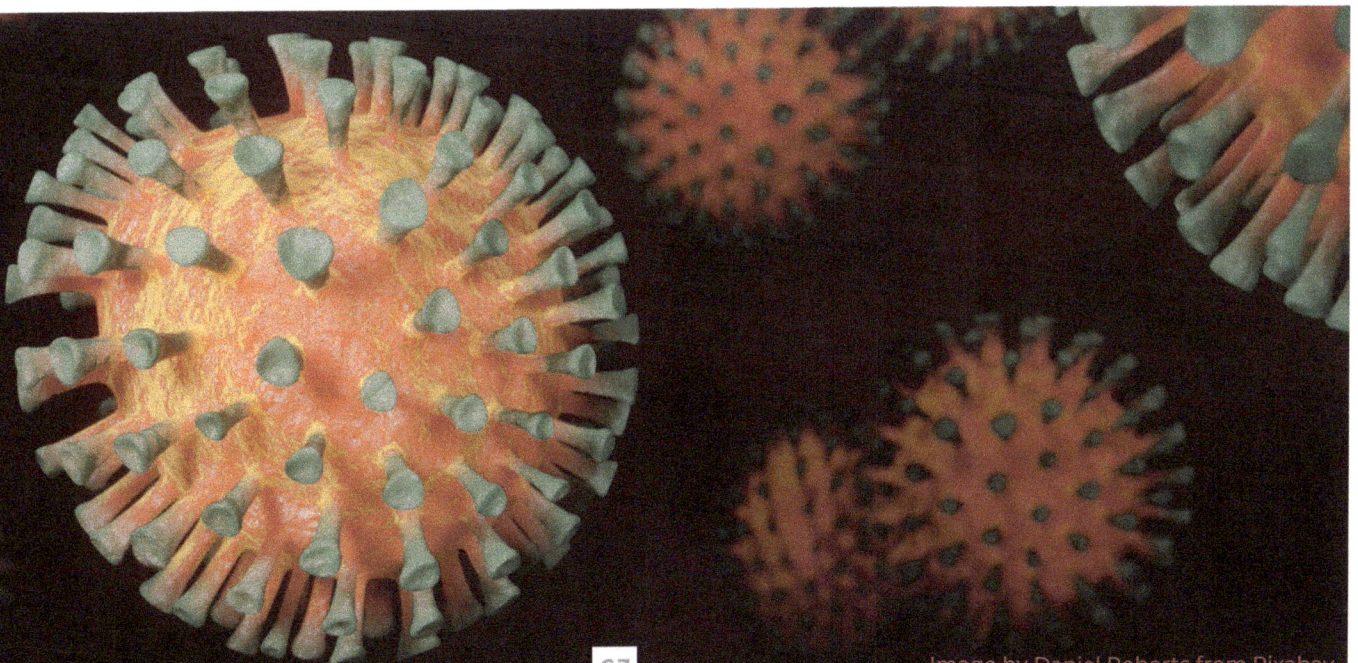

SCHOOL MEALS

SCHOOL MEALS

The School Breakfast Program (SBP) and the National School Lunch Program (NSLP) are federally assisted meal programs that provide meals in schools and residential childcare institutions. In Texas, the Texas Department of Agriculture administers the programs. All the San Antonio area ISDs administer the programs during the school year and in the summer (16). As the pandemic progressed, the Texas Department of Agriculture modified the state guidelines to overcome distribution and funding hurdles. ISDs adopted these changes and established the processes needed to implement them.

This section provides snapshots of the actions that school districts took to provide students with school meals during the first 60 days after the Governor's issuance of the in-person school closure.

North East ISD - 1,000,000 meals in less than two months were distributed to students starting with a curbside pickup model. "We know that almost half of our students depend on school meals for the majority of their nutrition during the day," said Sharon Glosson, Executive Director of School Nutrition. "School closures threatened the food access for these children. The NEISD meal program took one worry off parents' minds since they knew that their children would be provided with nutritious meals."

The program evolved to provide students with dinner and weekend snack packs. The School Nutrition Services worked with the Transportation Department to deliver the meals.

Schertz-Cibolo-Universal City ISD
Provided six sites for breakfast and lunch pick-up locations. Over 2,000 meals were served daily by the Child Nutrition Department and the Transportation Department.

Northside ISD
Child Nutrition Department staff assembled boxes for food distribution at 11 middle school sites. Middle and high school coaches, central office staff, school staff, police officers, and child nutrition staff teamed up to distribute over a million meals.

Partnered with the San Antonio Food Bank to distribute fresh produce and other food items to families.

South San ISD
Approximately, 152,578 free nutritious breakfast and lunch meals were distributed via a curbside service during the extended school break. Additional meals were sent home with students to provide them meals on days that the distribution sites were not open.

San Antonio ISD
Bus stop distribution operated Monday through Friday. This distribution included: meal bundles that contained breakfast, lunch, and supper for that day. Friday bundles included weekend meals.

DISTANCE LEARNING

DISTANCE LEARNING

Teachers and their support team faced the challenge of having to transition from in-school learning environment to a remote one basically overnight. While distance learning was not new to ISDs, the magnitude of the number of students, the scalability of applying it in the virtual learning environment, and the short implementation time-period were major barriers. Teachers responded quickly by recreating their lesson plans, communicating with students, and adapting to the extended usage of technology. To ensure students could operate remotely, ISDs distributed available end devices. They also supplement this distribution with technical support. Technology teams provided network access for students in multiple ways, including hotspots to students' homes, Wi-Fi enabled school buses parked in convenient areas, and boosting Wi-Fi signals at campuses which were accessible from the parking lot.

Distance learning opportunities and options extended beyond academics to include virtual support of athletics, fine arts, and other extracurriculars. This section provides snapshots of the actions that school districts took to provide students with distance learning during the first 60 days after the issuance of the in-person school closure.

Schertz-Cibolo-Universal City ISD
The technology department assisted families without internet devices needed for remote instruction. Approximately, 900 student devices (e.g., laptops and iPads) were distributed over a two-week period. There were over 190,000 logins through ClassLink from students in the one-month period between March 30, 2020-April 28, 2020.

South San Antonio ISD
An estimated 2,500 Google Chromebooks were distributed to students. Free hotspots were provided for families without internet service. Members of the district's IT team were also available to assist teachers and students with any connection concerns.

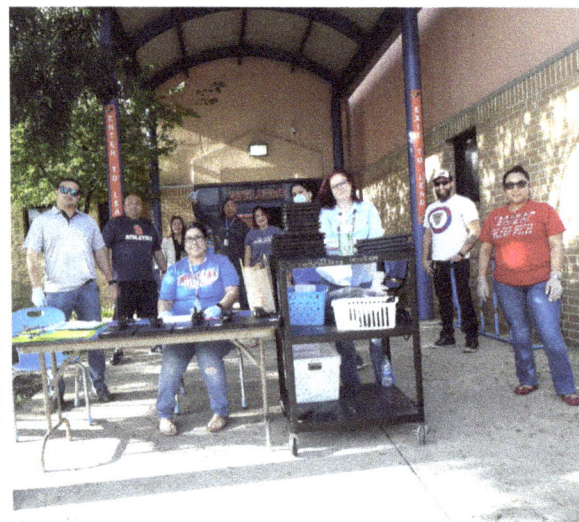

North East ISD

Distance Learning offered specialized curricula in English and Spanish. The website offered a one-stop shop for students in Pre-K, elementary, middle, and high schools with vast resources in every subject.

Northside ISD

A team of volunteers from across departments and campuses distributed thousands of computer devices and hotspots for students to use at home. Teachers used Google Classroom to offer distance learning for students. 10,000 devices were requested for home use.

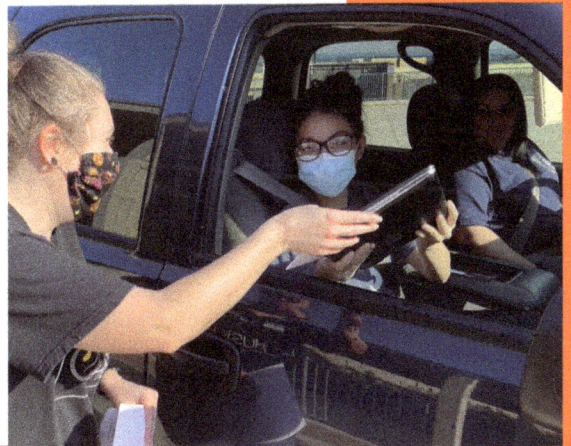

Southside ISD

Offered free internet and Wi-Fi for 60 days to all qualifying low-income households who did not subscribe to an internet service. Additionally, the internet provider agreed not to terminate the residential or business service if the customer was unable to pay the bill. The provider also waived late fees. Some cell phone data plan fees in the area were temporarily waived.

San Antonio ISD

Accelerated the strategic plan from a three-year strategy to a three-week goal to provide 1:1 technology across the District. Implemented emergency measures to acquire 30,000 devices (e.g., Chromebooks and hotspots), for home internet access. Earlier distributions to students involved the deployment of older devices that were in the inventory.

Updated Digital Learning Platform to include weekly messages for students and families. Provided a link where students could submit work in real time, experience virtual field trips, participate in STEM challenges, access a creativity corner, and engage in physical movement.

Lackland ISD

Communicated messages supporting disinfecting and cleaning surfaces. Emphasized the need to disinfect technology devices and provided step-by-step instructions on sanitation of devices for students, staff, and families.

COUNSELING

COUNSELING

Per the Texas Education Code, the primary responsibility of a school counselor is to counsel and fully develop each student's academic, career, personal, and social abilities. (17) This responsibility extends beyond the school settings. Therefore, when students were not allowed to attend in-person, ISDs immediately identified the plans and resources needed to continue counseling services for their students and their families. Counselors set-up call-in centers to provide students and families with emotional and psychological support. When necessary, counselors served students at their home residence and other locations.

This section provides snapshots of the efforts and plans implemented by the counselors to avoid disruption in essential services and learning.

Floresville ISD
Provided a partial listing to its students and families of the counseling services available to them. This list shows the depth and broadness of the counseling services provided by all ISDs. It included:

- Accommodations and modifications
- Auditory Services
- Special Education Counseling
- Occupational Therapy
- Physical Therapy
- Vision and O&M Services
- Speech Therapy
- Parent Communication

Photo by mentatdgt from Pexels

North East ISD

Launched a School Nurse Hotline for students and families to speak with a school nurse about their health questions and concerns. "Staying connected to people is what gives us our humanity," said Cindy Valadez, RN. "Sometimes, the nurse hotline is about sharing new information. Other times, it's about providing reassurance or simply giving someone a verbal hug. Our NEISD parents are receptive, appreciative, and gracious during our conversations. When you hear someone say thank you with their heart, that's victory!"

Established a Counselor Support Line for students and families to speak with a counselor about their academic and non-academic related questions.

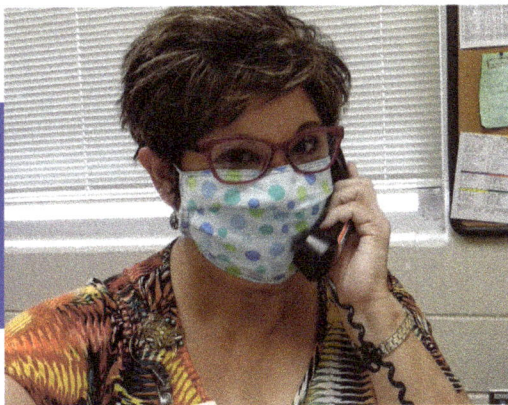

South San Antonio ISD

CARE Zone continued to provide food, clothing, and emotional support services in the community. Added a direct line to the CARE Zone to expedite requests for support.

Teachers put together distance learning packets and survival kits so their students could have hard copies of the lessons and to make sure the students knew their teachers were thinking about them.

COMMUNITY ENGAGEMENT

COMMUNITY ENGAGEMENT

ISDs became active supporter of their community through logistical support and by applying their creativity to overcome hurdles caused by COVID-19. Students, parents, and teachers made masks and PPE for first responders, nursing homes, and neighbors. Students also used their personal or borrowed 3D printers to make face shields for medical personnel. Districts donated their medical supplies, gowns, masks, etc.to hospitals needed to immediately get their PPE orders filled.

This section provides snapshots of the community support by ISDs during the first 60 days after the issuance of the in-person school closure.

North East ISD
Teachers, staff, students, and parents across several communities gathered together to take part in community parades.

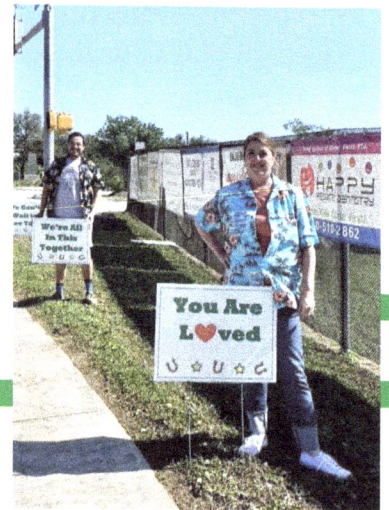

Ft. Sam Houston ISD
Kindergarten – second grade teachers modified the traditional "Flat Stanley" activity to create "Flat Teacher" pictures that encouraged students to take their "teacher" along on outings.

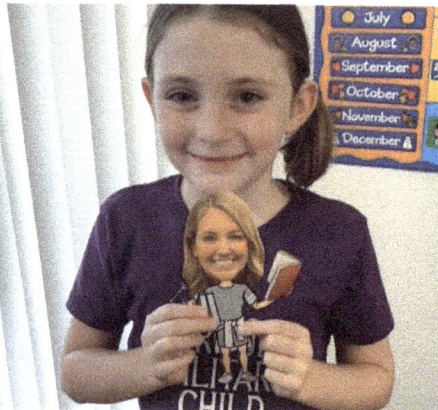

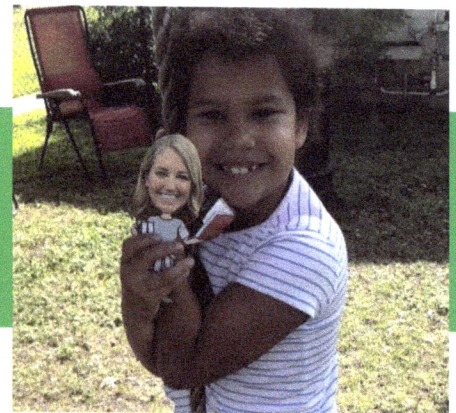

#FSHISDCookAnywhere was created to support culinary arts student instruction. Its impact expanded to encourage family wellness through healthy meals for students and teachers. It also showed respect and concern to those in the food service industry impacted by Stay Home orders.

Schertz-Cibolo-Universal City ISD

Teacher Appreciation Week, National School Nurse Day, and National School Lunch Hero Day were observed. Events were held to allow graduating seniors an opportunity to see teachers/mentors one last time.

Northside ISD

Secretaries responded to community questions and served as a voice for their campuses.

Custodians worked behind the scenes making buildings safe. They ensured all schools were stocked with cleaning supplies, including soap and dispensers, and that all areas were properly disinfected.

Stepped up to help local hospitals in the San Antonio area overcome the local and national shortage of personal protection equipment (PPE) by donating thousands of masks, gowns, and thermometers to the local hospitals. Established a precedence of support that was followed by other ISDs across Texas.

South San ISD

Provided educational and motivational support through the district's social media channels. These channels made it possible for school staff to reach out to students safely.

Medina-Valley ISD

The MVISD McKinney-Vento Program worked with families and unaccompanied (homeless) youth who lived in a temporary living situation due to the loss of their home.

The Medina Valley ISD Homeless Liaison helped families by working in partnership with the county government, as well as a network of service providers, food pantries, clinics, shelters, and numerous charitable organizations.

CHAPTER FOUR

GO PUBLIC

INTRODUCTION BY HANNAH GARCIA
Northside ISD High School Graduate and UTSA Student

"My collaboration with Go Public began when I was a junior at Communications Arts High School. Six years later, I can say with great pride that Go Public shaped my life.

I first worked on an independent documentary with Go Public. What started out as a school assignment became an eye-opening experience. I met educators and stakeholders across San Antonio whose passion was contagious. I became invested in the pro-public education message behind Go Public. Now, as a junior in college, I am studying Government and Education Policy and hope to support student education on a governmental level one day.

Go Public recognizes the wonderful teachers and faculty serving San Antonio public schools, two of whom are my parents. Go Public bridges our San Antonio community and advocates for equal opportunity for all students, everywhere. I feel this is something that everyone can get behind!

I am thankful to the Go Public leadership team for supporting me throughout my academic career and look forward to giving back with my contribution to this publication."

PHASE 1

GO PUBLIC LAUNCH

GO PUBLIC LAUNCH

Go Public is a collaborative, positive campaign promoting the great things happening in the San Antonio and Gulf Coast area ISDs. The campaign is overseen and managed by the ISDs' Boards of Trustees and Superintendents in both regions. In the San Antonio region, the legal and financial affairs of Go Public falls under the auspices of the Bexar County School Boards Coalition.

The campaign began as a result of two parallel conversations:

1. The San Antonio area Superintendents were concerned about and discussing the sudden expansion in the negative advertisement about public education by some charter systems
2. The San Antonio area Trustees were discussing the need for more parental and general public engagement in their ISDs.

The superintendents were concerned about the increase of blogs and marketing materials published by advocates of charter education in San Antonio. These efforts cast public education in a negative light. In parallel, San Antonio's increase in charter schools demonstrated a concerted effort to establish a strong presence of charters. The superintendents foresaw the damage this narrative would have on the relationship between families and the public education system, enrollment in ISDs, and the community's outlook on educational success.

The trustees recognized that parental involvement in their child's education was a major contributing factor to achieving the vision and goals of each ISD. They realized that expanded communications and messaging was needed to reach these parents and families.

G🍎 PUBLIC
LOVE YOUR SAN ANTONIO-AREA ISDs!

In 2013, the Superintendents and Trustees collaborated to address both of these concerns and set the foundation for what became the Go Public campaign. This formation was solidified when the San Antonio area ISDs passed and signed a memorandum of support at their school board meeting. To commence the operations, a steering committee comprised of Superintendents and Trustees convened to start the campaign.

• Branded the campaign as Go Public
• Created the logo and tagline
• Engaged Mike Baselice to conduct a survey to test which messages resonated best with the public
• Laid out a comprehensive advertising and digital marketing strategy that included a website, social media assets, various types of collateral, as well as radio, TV, digital, and outdoor advertising

To broaden the impact, the steering committee obtained support from the business community. Leaders from major corporations, including USAA and Toyota, served as campaign co-chairs. With new corporate leadership engagement in place, the steering committee then sought engagement from local bankers, architects, contractors, lawyers, accountants, foundations, nonprofits, and government organizations.

On November 8, 2013, Go Public officially launched with a press conference at Jefferson High School in the San Antonio Independent School District. The launch kicked off the indoor and outdoor promotion campaign including:

• 25,000 round "Go Public" magnets on vehicle bumpers all over town
• Television, radio, and digital ads ran in local media outlets
• Bus wrap advertisement on VIA buses during San Antonio Fiesta
• Outdoor billboards placed on major interstate thoroughfares and near facilities used for school graduation ceremonies

Through a survey of Bexar County residents, the steering committee and DeBerry Group determined the themes the public associated with the ISDs. The campaign messaging focused on the three most popular themes:

• Local public schools (i.e., ISDs) have the most experienced and longest serving teachers
• Students in local public schools have the best extracurricular opportunities such as sports, band, and clubs
• Local public schools help create a sense of community

Go Public's success was recognized early across Texas. The campaign received statewide recognition, including the Texas School Public Relations Association's Bright Idea Award for outstanding promotion of public education in Texas through effective communications.

PHASE 2

RESOURCES AND STORYTELLING

RESOURCES AND STORYTELLING

In 2016, the committee selected an Executive Director, Lisa Losasso Jackson, to further develop and manage the campaign. Lisa focused Go Public toward two important strategies: providing resources to parents and families and anchoring the marketing around storytelling. Lisa expanded the marketing and advertising efforts by amplifying the districts' successes through social media. She worked closely with TV and radio producers to develop unique programs that told compelling stories. Lisa dove deep into each of the ISDs, identifying an offering of 180 academic and extracurricular programs, collectively. The vast array of choices continues to serve as the anchor for all of Go Public's promotional and educational efforts.

Lisa and the steering committee recognized that partnerships and media buys with local TV stations would be the best outreach tool for storytelling, especially in highlighting the wide variety of choices. These initiatives included the following:

• Channel 12/KSAT's Cool School Program featuring students, teachers, schools, and the great activities in San Antonio-area's public schools

• Channel 4/WOAI's Go Public with David Chancellor featuring various heartfelt stories of students with compassion and care. In 2020, David received Texas School Public Relations Association's annual Media Award for the Go Public features

• Channel 35/CW's Thursday Night Lights recognizing outstanding teachers. This not only served to appreciate deserving teachers, but also demonstrated the commitment among public educators to providing an enriching and engaging classroom

Branded as "Go Public with Keyhla", Univision spots featured former ten-year anchor, Keyhla-Calderon Lugo, connecting on a deeper level with the Spanish-speaking populations. Univision launched a series of five commercials for both TV and radio. Go Public connected the campaign to the websit through an "En Español" page.

Critical to any marketing effort is its website. Go Public went through its first redesign in 2016 and a second one in 2020. New content included features guides, reports, and other materials to support parents and families in understanding the pathways and resources available to students. The existing website drives users to learn more about each ISD through their district profile pages. The profiles provide a succinct and concise reference including the district's mission and vision.

To support the variety of programs offered, each profile contains drect links to the district's specific website pages on programs like Pre-K, STEM, and special education. Additional topics and areas of focus include:

• Clarification of differences and similarities of public, private, and charter education
• School choice options, including magnet programs, academies, and STEM initiatives
• After school care
• Extracurricular activities, including athletics, JROTC and fine arts
• Academic advancement initiatives such as the dual-language and gifted and talented programs
• Career and Technical Education (CTE)
• Curriculum, college, and career checklists

Because of the complexity and competition of social media and a race to the top of any search on Google or other search engines, Lisa brought in part-time consultants and worked with them to achieve the goal of creating awareness and engagement around the ISDs' offerings, while maximizing TV, radio, and digital campaigns. The consultants specialized in building followers, driving traffic through SEO and keyword research, writing content, and leveraging search algorithms. The efforts succeeded in tripling the traffic on the Go Public website and social media within a year.

In 2020, Lisa and the consultants worked on a new vision for the website. The idea was to merge Go Public in San Antonio with the campaign in the Gulf Coast. This collaboration provided the opportunity to: produce a rise in Go Public's search rankings, increase in its domain authority, and compete better against the charter networks' efforts. Through an in-depth analysis of what charters were doing to dominate online searches about public education, it became increasingly clear that Go Public's website and content production were a strong tactic in educating the public. The site redesign included streamlining the regions, building out a school finder tool, and highlighting programs and services offered in public education. The goal of directing users to the ISDs' websites still serves as a central function of Go Public's site.

The Go Public campaign expanded the use of radio in 2020. This expansion included spots on Texas Public Radio, pop station 96.1 and Latino Hits 104.5. In addition to advertisements promoting the programs and parent resources, both 96.1 and 104.5's on-air talent provided live testimonials about the power of public schools. Since both were graduates from San Antonio area ISDs, their testimonials were anchored in enthusiasm and authenticity.

Go Public teamed up with three professional sports teams in San Antonio to recognize and celebrate public education within our ISDs.

Go Public Night with the San Antonio Missions included on field, pre-game first pitch, special tickets, t-shirts, logo on the scoreboard, and video on Jumbotron.

Go Public Night with the San Antonio Commanders included superintendent and trustee recognition, pre-game activities for students, special ticket pricing, and video on Jumbotron.

Go Public Night with the San Antonio Spurs included pre-game prizes, autograph opportunities, special t-shirts, and served as a fundraiser for Go Public.

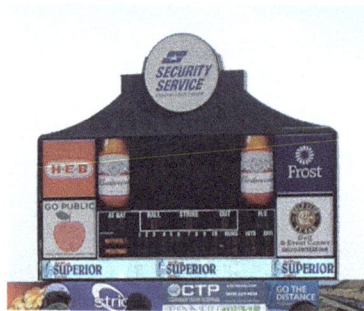

GO PUBLIC
LOVE YOUR SAN ANTONIO-AREA ISDs!

Go Public also participated in or partnered with other events which included:

Student Art Exhibit on City Buses, which connected art from public schools to the San Antonio Chamber and Texas Cavaliers.

Student artwork featured on billboards.

Heroes for Health connected 300 elementary schools, physical activity, and nutrition to San Antonio Fire Department, San Antonio Police Department, Bexar County Sheriff Office, Bexar County Constable, ISDs Police Departments, Volunteer Fire Departments, and the military.

YMCA partnership connected the community to Go Public's message

"Top Chef" style cook-off that connected Culinary Arts programs to the Culinary Institute of America, the Beef and Dairy Councils, and the restaurant association.

KSAT's Back to School Primetime Special was a bonus, value-added benefit for Go Public.

PHASE 3

GO PUBLIC EXPANSION

GO PUBLIC GEOGRAPHIC EXPANSION

Since its beginnings in 2013, Go Public has undergone important changes to expand its capacity to promote public education. Go Public has increased its partnerships with businesses, community members, and other pro-public education organizations. These connections have been crucial in securing sponsorships that maintain organizational expenses and build networks of support. Go Public has established partnerships over the past three years with organizations with similar initiatives, including RootEd, a nonprofit founded by parents with the mission of advocating for public education across communities, as well as with Friends of Texas Public Schools, and the Texas Association of School Boards. Like Go Public, these organizations can work together to strengthen their common goals.

The expansion into the Houston and Gulf Coast region shared a common mission with the San Antonio area Go Public but maintained local leadership and legal structures. By establishing chapters in other Texas communities, Go Public has grown in its geographic potential to inform parents, families, and community members on the successes of public education, increasing its impact.

WHY GO PUBLIC?

Public schools are a critical component of building stronger communities. By providing opportunity to all students, public education creates a new generation of productive and giving citizens, in turn, which results in a cycle of prosperity. Go Public advocates understand, however, that this cycle is limited when narratives dampen community support of public education.

Through sharing the incredible stories happening in our public schools, Go Public has made it a mission to correct this narrative and illustrate that ISDs are pathways to success for all students. Research shows that most millennials get their information online (18). Search engines like Google, social media, Facebook parent groups, and digital ads can influence how a school is perceived. The competition for clicks on an ad continues to grow as charter schools and school directories increase ad spends to reach parents who are searching for information.

In 2020, Go Public prioritized its online efforts including the merging of the Gulf Coast and San Antonio websites into one. The expansion of its school district finder map to a deeper level school finder, enables Go Public to attract more parents to its site, providing invaluable information about academic programs and services, and driving those parents directly to the ISDs. Go Public's small team is able to research and develop ongoing content that educates and promotes the value of traditional public schools. The success of Go Public is a direct result of its collaborative model. ISDs work closely with Go Public, providing access to success stories, innovative programs, and current data. In addition, the districts now have an additional resource in the grassroots efforts led by the parent volunteer organization, RootEd. The Go Public team works behind the scenes to support RootEd as they build parent representatives throughout the member districts.

Parents and families are faced with many choices when it comes to a child's education. ISDs, charter, private, and virtual educational pathways are all competing for enrollment. Go Public has solidified itself as a trusted source, working on behalf of and in coordination with, ISDs to amplify their efforts of promoting their offerings.

REFERENCES

1. Education Code, Title 2, Subtitle A., Chapter 4, Sec. 4.001
    Public Education Mission and Objectives.
2. Constitution of the State of Texas, Article VII.
    Education – The Public Free Schools, Section 1.
3. Education Code, Title 2, Subtitle C, Chapter 11, Sec. 11.002.
    Responsibility of School Districts for Public Education
4. Texas Education Agency Pocket Edition,
    Texas Public School Statistics and Education Code,
    and Title 2, Subtitle I, Chapter 45, Sec. 45.002 Maintenance Taxes.
5. Public Education Information Management System (PEIMS)
6. Enrollment in Texas Public Schools, Texas Education Agency,
    Division of Research and Analysis.
7. Enrollment in Texas Public Schools, Texas Education Agency,
    Division of Research and Analysis.
8. PEIMS Standard Reports, Texas Education Agency,
    Student Program and Special Populations Reports.
9. Enrollment in Texas Public Schools, Texas Education Agency,
    Division of Research and Analysis.
10. Interwoven Futures, Activating Strategic Alignment for Youth Success,
    Landscape Report 2020, UP Partnership.
11. Texas Education Agency Pocket Edition,
    Texas Public School Statistics and Education Code.
12. Texas Education Agency Pocket Edition,
    Texas Public School Statistics and Education Code.
13. Fiscal Notes: Texas School Finance: Doing the Math on the State's Biggest Expenditure.
    Comptroller.Texas.gov
14. Timeline of Coronavirus in San Antonio,
    San Antonio Express News.
15. Governor Abbott Declares State of Disaster in Texas Due to COVID-19,
    Office of the Texas Governor, Greg Abbott, Proclamation.
16. School Breakfast Program and National School Lunch Program,
    USDA Food and Nutrition Service, U.S. Department of Agriculture.
17. Education Code, Title 2, Subtitle F., Chapter 33, Sec. 33.006
    School Counselors; General Duties.
18. How Younger Generations Consume News Differently,
    Digital News Report, Antonis Kalogeropoulos, Research Fellow, Reuters Institute